The Uses of the American Prison

WITHDRAWN

The Uses of the American Prison

Political Theory and Penal Practice

Joan Smith
William Fried

Lexington Books
D.C. Heath and Company
Lexington, Massachusetts
Toronto   London

Library of Congress Cataloging in Publication Data

Smith, Joan, 1935-
The Uses of the American Prison.

Bibliography: p.
    1. Prisons—United States. 2. Rehabilitation of criminals—
United States. 3. Prison psychology. I. Fried, William, joint author.
II. Title
HV9471.S63   365'.973   74-294
ISBN 0-669-92775-9

Published simultaneously in Canada.

Printed in the United States of America.

International Standard Book Number: 0-669-92775-9

Library of Congress Catalog Card Number: 74-294

For George Jackson, the inmates in
Vermont and New Hampshire, and
our children all for whom he stood:
That they may live in a more just
society.

Contents

List of Tables

Acknowledgments

This book was made possible in part through a grant from the Spaulding-Potter Foundation and the Regional Affairs Program, Dartmouth College.

We would like to thank Donna Musgrove who both typed and edited the manuscript.

We would also like to thank all the people who were helpful in the relevant research projects at the New Hampshire and Vermont State Prisons. These include Randy Barber, Beverly Culver, Mary-Ann Kane, John Kugler, Tony Mueller, and Kerry Robertson. A greater debt is owed to the inmates we saw at those prisons who were most generous with their insights and information.

Finally, we must thank Rusti Eisenberg, Judy Jones, Marlene Gerber Fried, Richard Olsen, and John Kugler for their many vital criticisms and long hours of help. Without their assistance, what took years could have been accomplished in style in months.

Introduction

The social history and the modern condition of prisons can be described as responses to the interest of those in power. While this does not *necessarily* imply a conflict of interest between the few and the many, it does imply that every American prisoner today is incarcerated as a result of a political process. The extent to which this statement shocks is a measure of the degree to which the political aspect of punishment has been obscured.

The stress on the politics of law, its creation and enforcement has increasingly captured the attention of social scientists who had previously concentrated on the shared characteristics of individual transgressors. But this new focus on the politically determined aspects of our legal system has yet to permeate the study of the maximum security prison. Yet if these social scientists are correct in assuming that power and politics play a significant role in fashioning the criminal justice system, we must suspect that they play an equally important role in determining the structure and function of the end-product of the use of that system—the prisons.

While it may be argued that it is in everyone's interest to control the behavior for which most inmates are incarcerated, this does not obviate the fact that imprisonment itself results from the use of a system that is differentially available to whole segments of society. To the extent that this system is used to control actions whose reprehensible nature is generally agreed upon, the use of that system to enhance the interest of one group at the expense of another will be obscured and leave the impression that the legal system is democratic in results if not in structure. If the interest groups with dominant political control have a stake in controlling crime, they have an equal stake in convincing themselves and others that such control is exercised on the behalf of all.

This book examines the conditions under which prisoners and prisons come into being, change, and develop. A constant feature of these conditions is the economic environment within which doctrines of crime and punishment are expounded and penal practices evolve.

However, there is no linear relation between economic conditions and the theories and practices that constitute crime and punishment in a society. Rather, as economic conditions change, so will political conditions with their accompanying assumptions of what constitutes legitimate coercion for what kinds of activities. It will come as no surprise, then, that *criminal* procedures are almost universally reserved for behaviors in which the powerful obviously need not indulge. This is not to argue that those in power do not indulge in law-breaking activities but only that the most severe sanctions are brought to bear against acts that would be senseless were their perpetrators in a more secure position.

Crime and penal sanctions are always a feature of a political unit since by definition that unit is the outcome of competition over the right to define what is "deviant" and to "treat" its perpetrators. For crime to become a social reality—something perceived and treated as a failure in following legal criterion and thereby legitimately open to legal sanction exclusively at the hands of the state—valid assumptions must be in effect concerning the conditions upon which a citizen's political obligation rests.

Once the unit charged with apprehending and "treating" the criminal is seen as meeting the conditions which confer political legitimacy and demand political obligation, crime and punishment take on a reality totally different from what would be the case if those conditions were absent.

This is simply to argue that while the notion of crime makes reference to a certain kind of behavior, it equally and necessarily makes reference to claims of state authority. Minus that authority the behavior may be immoral but not criminal.

The general treatment of the criminal in the twentieth century, however, has obscured this relation between the inmate and the state by concentrating on features of the former to the neglect of the latter. While this tendency is slowly being eroded in the study of the creation of law and its enforcement, this newer position has yet to inform the analysis of the structure and functioning of the prison and the political uses to which punishment is put. The prevailing view is still that criminal behavior is descriptive of a kind of person rather than a kind of state. This view has enormous consequences for it imputes to criminal behavior some inherent quality independent of the needs or values of the powerful who, it is assumed, merely act as neutral guardians through the agency of the state on behalf of community-held values.

Moreover, by neglecting the political aspect of crime and punishment, one is led to uncritically assume as given that which stands most in need of exploration; the relation between political doctrine, state practices and doctrines of punishment. That this relation is real can be shown by an examination of changing conceptions of the criminal and changing doctrines of punishment. That this relation is important to the present dilemma of prisons and prisoners alike can be shown by examining how the current doctrine of crime is worked out in penal practice.

What we suggest is that the prison and its practices answer the twin needs of the state to express itself in a liberal doctrine of political legitimacy and obligation while indulging in practices that would otherwise negate that legitimacy and obviate that obligation.

In brief, what appears as chaos and mismanagement is more intelligible as a rational, if unstable, response to a tightly constraining set of social, economic and political parameters. The prison is as much a captive of its social milieu as the inmate is of his.

A Methodological Note

Any realistic theory of crime and its treatment must start with the general premise that the coercive function of the state and the doctrine by which it is realized are subject to historical transformation. Social scientists have tended to react to this lack of constant structure by granting that all sociological materials are culture-bound and then trivialising that insight by attempting corrections through either statistical manipulation or theoretical constructs. The vital point thereby ignored is the fact that any deductive system using crime as invariable data is defective from the outset—that is, without the politically produced ability to define, convict, and treat crime, the very materials with which the social scientist must begin are necessarily absent. This is not to say that crime as a gross behavior would not exist, but simply that it would not exist as crime.

While some have noted that fluctuations in the rates and kinds of crime are a product of what the state legislates as criminal, this insight has hardly altered their naturalistic approach to the treatment of crime. This approach manages to ignore the strange metaphysic whereby behavior once rewarded becomes viewed as sickness, mortal sins become misdemeanors, and *vice versa*. But rather than such changes representing a more methodological problem, they present us with a startling dilemma. For no small part of the "problem" of the prison is this tendency to analyze the treatment of crime as though it were a non-political, non-transitory endeavor. To the extent that the treatment of criminals is said to be based on objective, scientific principles, crime itself will be seen as "constant data," unaffected by the political, social, or economic milieu in which it occurs, is defined, and then treated.

Our stress will not be on the specific innocence or illegality involved in the incarceration and treatment of inmates, but on the general conditions of political obligation that make punishment possible and that are increasingly open to question. What we will insist is the following: The behavior for which most inmates are incarcerated would probably be counted by any normal person as wrong, yet it is not the "wrongness" of that behavior alone that puts the man behind bars but notions of what kind of "wrongness" the state can and should act upon. And this turns on the nature and extent of political obligation the state can expect. We will suggest that the state has, in most instances, abridged that political obligation of its citizens by producing a situation incompatible with the conditions that ground political obligation. The state has recognized this dilemma but, rather than confronting it, has simply redefined criminality in terms of mental, social, or biological pathology.

This last brings us back to the methodological problem of doing social science. For it is the social scientists themselves who have helped the state prove that crime is not inherently political in nature but rather an expression of some inner pathology, environmentally caused or physically produced. We have no doubt that these scientists have little use for state coercion, but their good motives do not save their work from being grist for the prison's mill. It is interesting to note that when civil authority was being most severely questioned, a scientific endeavor putatively free of political bias should produce precisely the findings that undergird the state's instruments of control. What begins as value-free ends up being politically useful precisely because of its "non-political" character.

The prison represents for us a set of social doctrines, which form the basic conceptual baggage used to organize and make rational the treatment of inmates, that make visible the character of the inmate and the license of the prison. That is to say, through doctrine, the inmate becomes a type of person who is admirably suited to the kind of rationale the state has found necessary in legitimizing its coercive activities.

The social scientist should know as well as anyone that what appears as the truth from a social point of view is necessarily a product of institutional arrangements. If this is true for the outside world where truth or falsehood are often matters short of life and death, in the prison the truth, validity, and legitimacy of what is happening to inmates and why are the first order of the day. If one assumes, for example, that prisoners are suffering from some type of psychological difficulty, this is a measurable hypothesis. If one argues that the criterion by which psychological difficulties are established is heavily tied to a given social order, then it is to the social order that one must direct one's attention.

What the prison does to whom and why speaks as much to doctrine as it does to the "facts." If we take this seriously, then each and every piece of data must be inspected not as a reflection of some real world but as a method for generating a real world within which the prison's idea of what is being done to whom and why meets doctrinal specifications.

Plan of the Book

This study attempts to account for some of the major factors that produce changes in doctrines of political obligation, how these in turn produce new theories of crime and punishment, and how these theories affect penal practices (Chapter 1). It then gauges the plausibility of the liberal doctrine of obligation which characterizes the modern state in terms of the actual practices of that state. It delineates those social and economic conditions that this doctrine must presuppose and compares them to modern conditions (Chapter 2).

In finding that there is a serious disjunction between the theory and practice of the modern state, it is suggested that the theory of punishment based on that doctrine will necessarily espouse contradictory claims and expectations for the behavior of those found "deviant." This contradiction produces a prison structure that has as its mandate the "reform" of the inmate and thereby "produces" an individual modeled on that which is appropriate to nineteenth-century liberalism rather than twentieth-century corporate capitalism. In short, the prison espouses the doctrine of liberalism in its practices while ignoring the social conditions that belie the theory (Chapter 3).

Since the *legal* relation between the offender and the state rests on questionable grounds, the state has increasingly turned to the assumption that crime is a "disease" thereby obscuring the politics of punishment. Prisons, therefore, have adopted as their stated goal the "treatment" of offenders. We would naturally expect that the structural arrangements of the modern prison would mirror those of other treatment-oriented organizations. We investigate this hypothesis and conclude that the control of members of these organizations and the professionals who treat them are totally absent in the prison and that, minus structural realignments, which would facilitate that control of members and thus accountability of staff, the prison as a social structure belies its claims of its goal of therapy. This raises serious questions concerning the plausibility of the new doctrine of punishment (Chapter 5).

If the prison is to maintain the appearance of a *legitimate* coercive institution, it must then show through its daily dealings with inmates that they suffer from a specific, inherent failure—that is, they are incapable of acting as the liberal individual who is inwardly constrained and outwardly free. The various rituals of inmate life can be fruitfully regarded as little ceremonies making evident their flawed character (Chapter 5).

In general, theories of rehabilitation, which are to supplant theories of punishment, have added to the coercive nature of penal institutions since they presume precisely what punishment forbids. In the prison, which is supposedly dedicated to both, the inmate finds rational behavior almost impossible, thus increasing his social visibility as an irrational person. This irrationality, however, is structurally produced rather than organically caused (Chapter 6).

Finally, we include an autobiographical account of a team of "helping professionals" within the prison. This account attempts to analyze the grounds of psychiatric care and how it must be coercive itself behind prison walls (Chapter 7).

The conclusion summarizes the implications of the theory of criminality and punishment that are expounded today. We suggest that the problems of the prison are in fact the problems of the total society. The prison, turned hospital, and the warden, turned doctor, do not address these problems but further obscure them.

The Uses of the American Prison

1

The Promise and the Reality of the American Prison

Why are certain methods of punishment adopted in one period only to be rejected in later ones? This question has been addressed by innumerable investigators, each of whom generally approach the topic by the wholesale adoption of a particular theory of crime or punishment. Thus, theories of revenge, restitution, and rehabilitation have been said to characterize penal methods in the Middle Ages, the Enlightenment, and the modern period, respectively. Depending on the position of the author, penal methods are described either within the context of the theory or are shown to be significantly different from that which the theory would lead one to believe. No matter what position is finally adopted, there seems to be almost a universal tendency to fail to account for the theory itself.

Certainly, it is neither self-evident that revenge is an appropriate way to describe practices of the Middle Ages nor that rehabilitation can be applied to those of contemporary society. In fact, the "treatment" model has been severely criticized by other authors but not along the lines we are proposing. We question what political order requires calling for such a model and not necessarily whether treatment actually occurs. The effectiveness of "treatment" can be, of course, a function of the former.

Modern critics of the penal system in this country have generally urged that penal practices significantly diverge from a penal theory that holds as its final goal the rehabilitation of the offender. Even the most radical of those who condemn modern practices do so from within the theory of rehabilitation and correction. There is little or no discussion in penal literature on the development of the theories that both supporters and critics alike use to legitimize their claims.

Seeking explanations for theories obviously has the taint of idealism—that is seeking for mere abstractions. However, because theory and practice diverge may be more, rather than less, of a reason to account for the theory.

The legal and penological categories of the modern system (responsibility, treatment, rehabilitation, and correction) are as much a part of the environment to which the inmate must respond as are his cell and bars. Together, they give his imprisonment its most salient characteristics. But little is made of these ideas; they stand as resources in describing the prison rather than as topics in their own right. Yet, these are resources of a recent vintage and were obviously not inevitable. What, then, accounts for their prevalence?

The present chapter is an essay in penal theories. But what it will attempt to show is that such theories are, in fact, products of political practices. It

1

suggests that the difficulties of our present system lie even deeper than even the most severe critics have noted; the political practices that have given rise to modern penal doctrine contain the central problem, which is the attempt to reconcile a theory suited to a market society with the realities of corporate capitalism.

For good reason, notions of criminality are not and cannot be independent of what constitutes political obligation, although this has generally gone unnoticed by both reformers and supporters of the present system. What we will show is that the prevalence of judging penal practices by criterion independent of political and economic activities implies an acceptance, whether deliberate or unconscious, of the inherent separation of the interests of the state and the treatment of its criminals. These tendencies of both humanitarian reformer and social scientist alike allow for the consideration of features of the criminal in abstraction from features of the state.

But there is a curious logic at work here, for it is obvious that notions of crime necessarily imply notions of political obligation. The term "political obligation", in turn, brings with it notions of a formalized legal body such as parliament or the legislature; however, we refer to those sets of behavior whose absence would allow the intercession of a *coercively* guaranteed law. The coercive apparatus, no less than the ability to make laws, does not always lie exclusively with the state [Weber, 1967, ch. 2].

The question, therefore, is what are the conditions under which the modern state claims political obligation to exist and which therefore legitimize the punishment of those who transgress? What we intend to show is that the *doctrine* that characterizes modern penal practices assumes particular conditions of political obligation that do not exist, and penal *practices,* in the absence of these conditions, can be understood as efforts to obscure the relationship between state and criminal by radically depoliticalizing the nature of crime and the role of the penitentiary.

Social scientists who would keep political practices and theories of punishment safely compartmentalized are facing a crisis at the hands of the very people they are seeking to help. According to the inmates' own protestations, they are no longer buying the terms of their imprisonment.

Quite often these inmates make an analogy between their situation and that of "natives" in the colonized part of the world. However, there is an important difference that is relevant to understanding the modern prison. In colonized countries, "the policeman and the soldier, by their immediate presence and their frequent and direct action, maintain contact with the native and advise him by means of rifle butts and napalm not to budge" [Fanon, 1963, p. 38]. In prisons, the atmosphere of force is generally a mere undercurrent: few guns are in evidence; the "custodians" patrol the yard, often alone and always unarmed. The notion of "correction" provides its own defense. Systems of rewards and benefits—the machine shop to learn a trade if you are a good "con," early release if you show signs of rehabilitation, the chaplain to care for your soul and the psychiatrist your head—all serve to create an atmosphere of care for the subjugated and thus lessen the burden of the brute fact of their subjugation.

As has often been pointed out by sociologists, the total institution is such that its very structure insures conformity [Goffman, 1961].[a] But as we will show with prisons, that structure must assume the presence of particular conditions, without which what might appear as authority and legitimacy would be revealed as brute force. Recent attempts to organize inmates and the more spectacular prison upheavals can be seen (whether by design or not) as demystifying this system and revealing the sheer force of the state behind the facade of "corrections." Without calling into account the very notion of "corrections" upon which the prison is putatively structured and upon which all but the most radical of critics would fashion a new system, an analytic insight into the structure and function of the modern penitentiary would be impossible.

Such an analysis is obviously timely since our prisons, one by one, are going up in flames. From the timid requests for better food and less crowding have emerged the more strident demands for a whole new "system." As one ex-convict urges:

> Political consciousness should be a priority in educating ourselves as well as our brothers and sisters. . . . Once we realize what we're dealing with, it is up to us to liberate ourselves and, in turn, help bring forth a political understanding, both in our prisons and on our streets. [*New England Prisoner Association News,* Nov. 1973]

Such changes in both the substance and style of demands should not lead us to the belief that they simply reflect either a different type of inmate (the radical or the drug freak) or deteriorating prison conditions [Mattick, 1972, pp. 13 ff.]. This argument seems to satisfy most liberal critics of the prison system. The danger, of course, with such arguments and what should lead us to suspect their objective validity is that prison administrators have a large stake in convincing themselves and the public that a certain kind of inmate causes all the trouble and that an increased budget will allow more efficient supervision of such inmates and at the same time remedy whatever conditions might also be at fault.

In one sense, the recent protest activities of prisoners *can* be compared to decolonization elsewhere—the process whereby the population once seen as rightfully subjected to alien rule questions the very grounds of their subjugation. But explanations of such militancy as being the product of a new kind of

---

[a]The problem of Goffman's work as with many others in the same *genre* is that there is little or no effort at analyzing the social conditions that must be present for the genesis of such structures. It is precisely these conditions that are required to be at least presumed to be present before such structures can "work."

convict ignore the essential historical transformation of prisons in the United States and abroad. Movements that set out to change the order of the world, as Fanon pointed out some time ago, are obviously going to appear to the observer without historical perspective as a program of complete disorder or chaos:

> Decolonization [read prisoner liberation] . . . cannot become intelligible nor clear to itself except in the exact measure that we can discern the movements which gave it historical form and content. [Fanon, 1963, p. 36]

It is this historical form and content of "correctional" institutions to which we now turn for an understanding of the modern maximum security prison.

The Sources of Prison Reform

It has become a convention in tracing the development of the penitentiary to begin with those "high-minded Pennsylvania Quakers who set about the abolition of . . . (barbarities in the treatment of the criminal) from the New World" [Mitford, 1973, p.30; see also Rothman, 1971, p. 80 FF.]. This convention at best leads us astray for it assumes that the modern prison doctrine is understandable as a revolt against penal practices that were prevalent in another setting and had no place within the revolutionary context of the New World. One recent author said, for example:

> [T]hat prison as a place of confinement [is] an institution of purely American origin, conceived by its inventors as a noble humanitarian reform befitting an Age of Enlightenment in the aftermath of a revolution against ancient tyrannies. [Mitford, 1973, p. 30]

This account is of course historically incorrect. Bentham was to design his penitentiary decades before the construction of the first penetentiary in the United States. That England chose not to construct one was more an effect of the opening up of Australia, which could be profitably colonized by convicts, than of any other factor [Shaw, 1966, chs. 1 and 2].

Far from being a purely American product based on humanitarian instinct alone, prison reform—or what has passed for prison reform—was not solely a triumph of humanitarian principles (no matter how humanitarian the individual reformers) but of changing productive relationships that in turn required new justifications of both the state and law. Far from the Pennsylvania reformers acting in a political and economic vacuum—which such arguments invariably lead one to believe—their drive to establish a new system for the treatment of society's problems is a direct result of those factors that coincided with the development and legitimization of the political basis of their society. For it is the case that a shift in notions of what constitutes legitimate authority and thus coercion is necessarily accompanied by a shift in justifying the treatment of those charged with transgressing against that authority. The authority for establishing the state in the New World is not a product of that world but of political assumptions that were native to England and the continent.

Such an assumption of the radical nature of the American Revolution and therefore the radical nature of its institutions serves a specific political purposes, even though those who make the argument certainly do not necessarily espouse that purpose. The fact is that the argument obscures the actual historical context—that is, the liberation of a rising entrepreneurial class within which crime takes on the garb of being an insult to the state. By accepting the notion that revolutions in penal practice speak to the new American state and the principles of humanitarianism espoused by that state, the changing conceptions of political authority and thus abuses to that authority are left out of consideration. If humanitarianism is a sufficient cause for social change, we would be living in a Utopia. Since we are not so living, it becomes necessary to ask what the social conditions are within which humanitarian instincts take particular forms and come into play.

The study of criminal treatment cannot be undertaken without noting what, in a particular time and place, was seen as "criminal" behavior. In order to explore the connection between crime and punishment, we cannot be guided by what we "know" of criminality. None of the concepts of our present system can play an organizing role in accounting for that system. The history of penal methods is essentially the history of those practices that are not only intended to separate the deviant from the normal but are also historical and necessarily political processes. In the present, it is taken for granted that certain classes of behavior automatically involve the state; it becomes the injured party and thus the institution responsible for the treatment, punishment, or even forgiveness of the offender.

Obviously the state has a very heavy stake in this assumption. But the fact is that such assumptions are a consequence of major historical changes—changes that are also coincident with fluctuating notions of legal justice and the treatment of criminals. If we accept such assumptions as given, we necessarily fail to see such changes for what they are. A practical consequence of this failure would be to forevermore obscure the historical roots of American prisons. As Kuhn [1970] has pointed out in another context, major revolutions in theoretical perspectives take place when prevailing preconceptions no longer adequately explain observed reality. What we would add to this observation is that, with regard to prisons, such revolutions take place when they are no longer consistent with the political basis of the society.

The Political Basis of Reform

Treatment of transgressors has been a factor of group life for as long as history has recorded that phenomena. The history of such treatment—its practice and theory—derives from the way groups conceptualize themselves and what, therefore, constitutes a threat to their ideologies. Legitimatizing the political basis of group life occurs in a framework that necessarily includes ideas concerning the way man organizes economic activity. Attitudes toward social miscasts (whether they be the sick, the insane, or the criminal) cannot then be treated apart from systems of production and the productive relationships they entail. Yet it is also true that they can neither be treated in historical abstraction, for actions and reactions have, in one way or another, brought us to the present.

If it is true that "every political revolution brings with it its own criminal legislation" [Radzinowicz, 1966, p. 6], it is equally true that it also brings with it its own notions of what to do with criminals. A political revolution consists not only in a change in the people in government, but the principles by which they govern. Secondly, these principles are understandable as an historical reaction to the system of government that went before. Thirdly, changes in power relationships are a function, at least in part, of new needs of the ascendent group—that is, given changes in material conditions, not only will new groups emerge, but they do so precisely because the very terms of power need be consistent with these new conditions. The effect of these three interacting historical elements is to produce a change in what is seen as constituting criminal behavior and thus what should be done to those guilty of such acts. When the administration of criminal procedures undergoes radical change, three factors are almost invariably present. The first is an increase in the political security of the ascendent group. The second lies in increasing centralization of that power, and the third and most important is a new administration based on the fiscal interests that correspond to the change in productive relationships.

It has been argued elsewhere with specific reference to the American system that "understanding of the causes of deviant behavior [leads] directly to the invention of the penitentiary as a solution" [Rothman, 1971, p. 79]. While this is technically correct, it is so only in the most trivial sense. For what an act is (a sin or a crime) dictates what treatments are appropriate and which institution is responsible for that treatment. If misdeeds are an offense against the state, this implies a very definite conception of the state—its legitimate role and its basis for claims of legitimacy. While thievery in the Western World may always have been considered misconduct, the kind of misconduct it was and therefore the kind of person who would indulge in it is a function of conceptions of legitimate authority. The nature of crime, then, and thus ways of *both* "explaining" it and "treating" it are *absolutely* political in nature.

If legitimate coercion is based on religion, those who are coerced will be called sinners. If legitimate coercion is justified in terms of a rational legal system, the coerced will be called criminals, and, as in the present, if coercion is legitimatized within the rhetoric of the behavioral sciences—that is, if wrongdoing is a function of psychological and environmental factors—then the coerced will be called sick. In this case, as so many others, how we label a thing is determinate of how we treat it. Reclassification of transgressors is then best explained not so much in terms of what they "really" are—sinners, criminals, or the sick—but in terms of the needs of particular political systems to extract obedience to themselves.

Prison "reform" and theories of deviance and its treatment must be seen as an interrelated and explicable whole set in the context of the requisite justifications of a legal system that would be consistent with the productive organization of the community. In each and every period of prison reform, reformers create the illusion that a specific penal practice is bound up with a specific penal theory *exclusively*—a theory which is unique to prisons—and it is, therefore, sufficient to demolish the theory in order to change the practice. But penal doctrine here is imbued with an independence and power that has always been illusionary [Murphy, 1973]. As we shall show, the theoretical innovation in which reform movements originate are the expression of an already accomplished change in the political, economic, and social complexion of the society.

The Middle Ages

The study of the historical roots of penal methods necessarily begins in the Middle Ages, for the later innovations that were to result in the modern penitentiary cannot be understood apart from that to which they were a reaction. The current notion that prisons *per se* were the invention of the Enlightenment is simply fiction. Wherever the notion of legal jurisdiction appears in Europe, there also appears some form of prison. By the eighth century, the notion of private jurisdictions began to emerge, and the private franchise holder invariably came equipped with a jail into which wrongdoers were thrown either for later trial or immediate punishment. (Thorstein Sellin estimates that the precursor to modern penal systems can be found in the monastic prisons of the Middle Ages where it was common to have cells for the "correction" of transgressors through penance and labor [Sellin, 1926, pp. 104-112]).

As early as the fourteenth century, commitment to jail was a common part of statutes governing vagrancy:

... every man and woman, of what condition he be, free or bond, able in body, and within the age of threescore years, not living in merchandize

nor exercising any craft, nor having of his own whereon to live, nor
proper land to occupy himself, and not serving any other, if he in
convenient service (his estate considered) be required to serve, shall be
bounded to serve him which shall him require. . . . And if any refuse,
he shall on conviction of two true men . . . be committed to goal till
he find surety to serve.
And if any workman or servant, of what estate or condition he be,
retained in any man's service, do depart from the said service without
reasonable cause or license, before the term agreed on, he shall have
pain of imprisonment. [Chambliss, 1973, p. 431, quoting from early
English Statutes]

The most striking fact about these statutes is that the vagrant can be committed
"on conviction of two true men." In short, the process whereby he goes to jail
is through private individuals who are *convinced*. Other crimes (if we can use
the word without inbuing it with the connotations of a more recent period)
were looked upon as acts of war to be repressed by private individuals, not by
any constituted authority [Kennedy, 1970, p. 6].

Procedures characteristic of the period reflected the accepted theory of
society and social relationships.

Society was interpreted . . . as held together by a system of mutual,
though varying, obligations. Social well-being exists . . . insofar as each
class performs its functions and enjoys the rights proportioned thereto . . .
Clearly this . . . doctrine is a . . . reflection of the feudal land system. . . .
Not less clearly the . . . doctrine of economic ethics is the expression
of the conditions of medieval industry. [Tawney, 1954, pp. 29–30]

Political obligation was, then, to one's own position in a natural hierarchy.
"Baptized by the Church, privilege and power became office and duty" [Tawney,
1954, p. 28]. Hence, crime was an expression of an unnatural obliteration of
the duties and privileges—class distinctions. Its "treatment" was naturally geared
toward re-establishment of those relationships. The serf or villain who was
charged with a crime would not have faced a public prosecutor but a private
individual who claimed to have been harmed, and it was to him that the serf
owed penance. Inability to pay the penance would quickly land the serf in
prison.

But it was the serf's master who would exact the punishment since the
former's total subjugation necessarily extended to the latter's right of punishment. If the lord failed to take appropriate action, he would find himself being
charged by his neighbors with a serious transgression.

Perhaps the most common prison of the period was that of the bishops
who not only had exclusive punitive jurisdiction over members of the clergy but
also over certain kinds of crime. By 1261, it became obligatory for each dio-
cesan to have a prison in the diocese; for example:

> The ecclesiastical courts claimed to deal with cases of breach of con-
> tract in general, on the ground that they involved *laesio fidei,* and with
> usury in particular, as an offense against morality specifically forbidden
> by the canon law. [Tawney, 1954, p. 50]

All is not so simple, however, since even prior to the reformation, ecclesiastical and secular authorities invariably contended for jurisdiction over commercial morality.

> The question at issue was not whether the userer should be punished—
> a point as to which there was only one opinion—but who should have
> the lucrative business of punishing him, and in practice he ran the
> gauntlet of all and of each. [Tawney, 1954, p. 51]

Sometimes the unresolved issues of a day are more instructive than one
might suppose. That the church had to do battle with secular local authorities
over the right to punish offenders does not obscure or deny the fact that the
dispute itself was seen as legitimate, regardless of which side one took. And
there is no question that the church was seen as having a legitimate claim on
the corporal punishment of transgressors. It was not a matter of a failure to
comprehend the difference between social and moral transgression, since this
is a distinction of a decidedly different period. Rather, it was a question of
within whose jurisdiction particular "crimes" fall.

A second but related feature that distinguishes punishment during this
time from later periods is that the treatment of offenders was a direct—and
self-conscious—effect of class position[b].

> Penance was carefully graded according to the social status of the
> evil-doer and of the wronged party. . . . The inability of lower-class
> evil-doers to pay fines in money led to the substitution of corporal
> punishments in their case . . . for example, a Sion Statute of 1338
> provided a fine, if the offender could not pay he was to receive corporal
> punishment by being thrown into prison and fed on bread and water.
> [Rusche and Kirchheimer, 1939, p. 9]

The assessment of fines or corporal punishment depended on one's capacity
to pay (and one's estate privileges). For example, the vagrant and the slave
almost always received some form of corporal punishment for obvious economic
reasons. Statutes covering crimes that were considered to be associated with the
lower classes were almost always accompanied by corporal rather than monetary

---

[b]". . . the 'right' of the individual consists, sociologically seen, in the mere probability
that the members of his kindship group will respond to their obligation of supporting his
feud and blood vengeance (an obligation guaranteed by fear of the wrath of supernatural
authorities) . . ." [Weber, 1967, pp. 19–20].

punishments. Further, the class of the individual offended against was a determining factor in the calculation of the degree of wrong.

This differential treatment of classes and the universally held notion that particular kinds of crime fell within various jurisdictions corresponds to and reflects assumptions commonly held concerning the degree and kind of obligation one had to be a kind of society. Society represented the natural and Godly order of things, and personal obligation was to this order. Crime, then, was anything that disturbed that order. The basis of this system was the land, and basic to landowning was the serf and the villain without whom the productivity of the land would be in serious jeopardy. Class privilege, class oppression, exploitation, and serfdom are all expressions of some larger plan:

> Society, like the human body, is an organism composed of different members. Each member has its own function, prayer, or defense, or merchandise, or tilling the soil. Each must receive the means suited to its station and must claim no more. [Tawney, 1954, p. 27]

The notion of personal responsibility to a centralized state played no role in this drama, since it was the totality of social relationships upon which the society functions. There was no notion of limits to obligation; they were all-embracing and unconditional.

And this is precisely what is to change, precisely what will usher in a new era in penal doctrine and methods. But before we get there, there is another part of the story that is necessary in understanding the Middle Ages. While one could be thrown in jail for indeterminable periods for the most minor of infractions, there were certainly mitigations available. These included the ordeals that were used to determine the guilt or innocence of a person accused, sanctuary, and compurgation. It is important to note that each of these imply the invocation of miraculous guidance in the determination of the guilt or innocence of a person and the degree to which he should be punished once found guilty. If all else failed, the accused could appeal either to the church or to the crown for pardon.

The point for us here is that it was precisely the *mitigations* available rather than the horrid lot of the offender that first came under attack. For example, in addition to attacking the system of private restitution of harms, the reformers of the latter part of this period expended their greatest energy on the royal prerogative to either pardon or annul sentences. While such pardoning was obviously abused, an historian viewing the period in perspective pointed out that the right of pardon was in part "a kind of antidote against the harshness of the prevailing penal system."[c] [Rusche and Kirchheimer, 1939, p. 16]

---

[c]It is not difficult to see that such a practice . . . was regarded with disapproval by the rising middle classes in their struggle for greater stability and rationalization of Government [Rusche and Kirchheimer, 1939, p. 16].

To our modern eyes, escape from punishment could seem rather irrational at times, and if escape was not forthcoming, the punishment itself could appear bizarre.

> These were the spontaneous reprisals with which the community strove to repay the criminals in kind . . . a baker who sold loaves which were short of weight was shown with the bread tied around his neck. A fishmonger who had been selling bad fish was paraded with a collar of stinking smelts slung over his shoulder. A grocer who had been selling much-adulterated spices was placed in the pillory and had the powders burned beneath his nose. [Ives, 1915, p. 112]

But the qualities with which we might characterize both the legal system and the system of punishment during this period—irrational, incalculable, or bizarre—are precisely those for which we are seeking an explanation. If the task is to establish the conditions under which penal doctrine undergoes significant change, the invocation of what are essentially elements of a later period to characterize practices in the former is at best tautological.

By the end of the sixteenth century, penal methods had undergone an enormous change. It has been argued elsewhere that these changes were a result of "certain economic developments which revealed the potential value of a mass of human material completely at the disposal of the administration" [Rusche and Kirchheimer, 1939, p. 24]. While this might be true, it does not explain the changes in political doctrine that allow for the wholesale congregation of prisoners in one place and under one jurisdiction—organized servitude. Galley slavery, deportation, and penal servitude, all innovations of the sixteenth century [Shaw, 1966, ch. 1], require a centralized administrative agency that is seen as *legitimately* the sole proprietor of civil order and thus the exclusive agent of punishment. We are not arguing that the town and church councils at this time did not still maintain this authority as well; rather, the period is marked by an increase in the power of the crown to exact punishment at the expense of these other agencies. By the later Middle Ages, two factors had produced a change in the "private character" of early medieval criminal law.

> One lay in the increasing prominence of the disciplinary function of the feudal lords. The only limit to the exercise of this disciplinary power was a jurisdictional claim by another lord. The second factor was the struggle of the central authorities to strengthen their influence by extending their judicial rights. [Rusche and Kirchheimer, 1939, p. 10]

In short, as we move into the sixteenth century, law takes on a decidedly "modern" flavor in that the coercive apparatus became the exclusive province of a political administration. Sovereign power was the necessary condition for

this evident change in penal methods; that penal methods then employed enhanced that power does not by any means indicate that such enhancement was
the *cause* of the change. It is evident that as nationalism became the movement
of the day there would be assumptions that not only legitimatized a strong
nation–state but also resulted in penal doctrine consistent with the needs of the
monarchy.[d]

The description of this transformation has taken up volumes. Suffice it to
point out that the new *penal* doctrine was a result of a mere skirmish compared
to the main battle that produced it. That battle was between the aristocracy,
the crown, and parliament, each of whose wealth was no longer a product of old
property relations but of buying the labor of others. Insofar as this was the
case, it implied two things: That social conditions were such that men were now
free to sell their labor, and economic conditions were such that they were *com-
pelled* to sell it. In short, the paternalistic model, which describes mutual obligations between lord and serf, must be replaced by a model that is more consistent
with market relationships, which in turn are preconditions for the emerging
nationalism. To postulate the ethical quality of these new market relationships
is to insist that there is a principle of equality that feudal society did not recognize; an equality of ability and of want rather than mere equality in the eyes of
God.

> In hierarchical societies the danger of slave or peasant revolts or popu-
> lar equalitarian movements is never entirely absent. As long as such
> movements are thought to be anarchical, thinkers who are constructing
> theories of political obligation must assume some functional or moral
> inequality between classes of men, for hierarchical society requires
> unequal rights and obligations. [MacPherson, 1962, p. 89]

By the end of the sixteenth century, new economic conditions required a
free labor market, which in turn required a wholesale dismissal of the notion
that political obligation is based on a Godly ordained hierarchy of social and
economic position. A centralized political force that will act as a control on
these mundane affairs will necessarily result in a centralized administration of
law. That the law was used in the services of that force should hardly be surprising.

Rusche and Kirchheimer [1939, p. 55] report one letter of 1676 from the
monarch to the Paris Parlement:

> Since His Majesty urgently needs more men to strengthen his rowing
> crews . . . to be delivered at the end of the following month, His

---

[d]Rusche and Kirchheimer's excellent work suffers from the assumption that penal
methods change as a *direct* result in changes in economic conditions. This unilateral model
of social change is deceptive since it treats the state, law, and doctrine as mere ideological
trappings.

Majesty commands me to tell you that He wishes you to take the necessary steps in his name in order to have the criminals judged quickly.

And the court responds:

You have frequently done me the honor of writing to me in connection, with the supply of prisoners for the galleys and of transmitting
to me the express orders of His Majesty relating to the use of such
prisoners in execution of his glorious projects. You will be gratified
to learn that this Court has twenty prisoners who will be chained
together this morning and sent off.

Similarly, the transportation of criminals was a method of punishment
made necessary by colonial expansion. But the expansion itself was based on
notions of the legitimate role of the nation–state and the political obligation
thereby entailed. Thus, the order that granted reprieve of the death sentence
for robbers and felons in favor of their being transported to the colonies
mentions that such penal servitude correct prisoners by "providing profitable
service to the Commonwealth in parties abroad" [Rusche and Kirchheimer,
1939, p. 56].

The outlook of the medieval middle-class intent on the conserva-
tion of corporate and local privileges [contrasts] . . . with that of the
new plutocracy of the Sixteenth Century, with its international
ramifications, its independence of merely local interests, its trium-
phant vindication of the power of the capitalist to dispense with the
artificial protection of gild and borough and carve his own career.
[Tawney, 1954, p. 68]

Whereas sovereignty in a feudal society was fragmentary, decentralized, and
based upon spiritual guidance, so were its notions of crime and treatment. With
the sixteenth century changes in economic conditions and material necessity,
sovereignty was to be marshaled as were the economic energies upon which it
depended. As much as this movement in history had to dispel the notions of
obligations characteristic of the earlier feudal period, it had to replace them with
assumptions of political obligations consistent with the system of this later
period. These assumptions in turn not only provided a new doctrine of the
right of centralized authorities to determine and treat crime but also the terms
in which such methods would be applied.

The Law and the Rational State

While we have argued that the needs of those in political power determined
how inmates were to be used, it is equally clear that the centralization of criminal

treatment is not so grossly economically determined but also speaks to the doctrines of political obligation that replaced those of an earlier era.

By the seventeenth century, "houses of correction" were to be found everywhere as wholesale internment became the order of the day. However, it is not the sophisticated brand of internment that we have come to know in our own time. By the end of the seventeenth century, the prison sentence as such became a general part of the criminal law, and although vaguely formulated, it provided for complete judicial discretion.

During that century the inscription above the House of Correction of Leipzig bore the following motto: "Improbis coercendis et quos desireit sanae mentis usura custodindis" (In order to correct the dishonest and to guard the lunatic). The statistics of the Ludwigsburg "prison" were common for most institutions of that time. Of the 283 inmates in 1780, less than half were convicted convicts; the others were orphans, paupers, or lunatics [Rusche and Kirchheimer, 1939, p. 65].

Thus, the dependent, the sick, and the disabled were generally to be found in the same institutions as were the criminal, all had little idea how long they would remain, for while there was no distinction made in treatment between classes of insults to the moral sensibilities of society, there was the additional element of incalculability in the degree to which those found guilty were actually made to suffer. In fact, it was felt by legal scholars of the day that a too tight statement of the punishment that attended particular kinds of offenses would weaken the deterrent value of that punishment.

Up to the end of the eighteenth century in the colonies, in England, and on the continent, most statutes that mentioned prison did so only as was necessary to secure payment of a fine, send a man into penal servitude, or hold him for whipping. In relation to colonial law, "the court would [generally] order a convicted defendant to be committed until all parts of the sentence were performed. . . . Imprisonment was often used to compel security to enforce the payment of fines or restitution" [Goebel and Naughton, 1944, pp. 516, 688]. Commitment to hard labor—transportation for work on the shipping hulls in Great Britain—required removal of the defendant from society. The removal itself was seen merely as a necessary artifact of the actual punishment.

If the prison was only a necessary concommitant to other coercive measures in the seventeenth and eighteenth centuries, by the end of that period there was no doubt that prison was a coercive measure in itself. The establishment of penitentiaries in America, to be followed almost simultaneously in Great Britain, was an immediate effect of transforming a means to an end in itself. While there were specific differences between and within countries, whatever the source of social deviation, it resulted in a policy of internment. This is a direct contradiction of Rothman's [1971] position. We can only suggest that by limiting his analysis to the United States, Rothman can conclude that a general policy of internment was a product of Jacksonian reform. But, as we argue, internment has a much longer history than that. Rothman apparently confuses *internment* with the rationale *for* internment, which does undergo significant change.

Of note for us is the fact that subsequent reformers in no way question the policy of internment. What was questioned was the calculability of internment; the *procedures* used rather than the outcome of the procedures. And such pleas as were made were not always made in terms of pure humanitarian motives but expediency. Sir William Meredith's call for a committee to consider capital offenses in 1770 was typical of his time:

> In a well-regulated state nothing is more requisite than to proportion the punishment to the crime, and thereby satisfy the mind of the people that equal justice is administered to every delinquent. At present, however, the crimes of larceny and petty theft, as well as of treason and murder, are alike punished with death . . . *from seeing the number of criminals that are pardoned, people are induced to commit offences under the idea that they can do so with impunity.* [Fletcher, 1939, p. 190; italics added]

The mitigation of harsh penal laws was to be expedited by "a strict and conciliatory attention to the morals and health of prisoners and [by] introducing a system of solitary confinement for certain crimes and establishment of penitentiary houses" [Fletcher, 1939, p. 196]. In establishing the act which was to bring such notions under law, Eden was supported by such famous reformers of the prison system as Blackstone and John Howard, both promoters of the scheme of penetentiaries in the eighteenth century [Fletcher, 1939, p. 196].

A close examination of the works of either Montesquieu or Beccaria, who had become by the close of the eighteenth century the princes of penal reform, reveals very little on the actual *conditions* of internment and a very great deal on the condemnation of a criminal justice *system* that was not governed by fixed and therefore calculable laws. Hardly a word is said about the actual, concrete contents of the system.

In short, the arguments of the reformers can be read as a call for a kind of state rather than a change in the actual treatment of convicts. And the need for a rationally organized state spoke more to the needs of a rising entrepreneurial class than to the actual conditions of the convict. The cries for a rational legal procedure are more coincident with economic necessities than the objective conditions of the destitute, criminal or insane.

What were these necessities? Briefly, with the growth and rapid expansion of textiles, mining, and especially foreign trade came an increased demand for a money market, stable credit rates, and a political order that would insure security for vast money transactions. Where notions of "good conscience" and "charity" may have been adequate safeguards in a highly personalized economic situation, it is apparent that the greater the distance and more complicated the transaction, the less compelling were such factors. It was the rising merchant class that caused, noticed, and acted upon the inverse relationship between conscience and opportunity—charity and profit—and hence led to the "discovery" of impersonal mechanisms governing large-scale transactions. That these mechanisms were precisely those that would, under the circumstances, increase the degree and security of profit generally went unnoticed. Accordingly, it was argued that both public policy and law should be congruent with impersonal forces of the market place. That those forces insuring the growth of capitalism were given the status of *inherent* psychological principles governing the behavior of all men tells us more about the material needs and ideological scope of the new entrepreneurs than about any self-evident, "natural" laws of human behavior.

Any state that interfered with these "natural" laws of the market or the psychological propensities of man to seek his own greatest profit as a free or spontaneous creator of his own life, it was argued, had no legitimate right to govern. The previous treatment of the socially deviant was viewed as a remnant of feudalism inimical to the interests of the rising middle class. Quite simply put, changes in such practices simply should flag for us fundamental changes in notions concerning the state, its grounds of legitimacy, and its boundaries.

Today, crime and punishment are considered products of the state. Without the power to legislate, behavior that we now refer to as crime would no doubt surely exist, but the ability to judge it a harm against the state and thus punishable exclusively by the state would be impossible. Thus, punishment by the state and the restitution such punishment implies require a theory of political obligation that is based on a very modern notion of citizenship—that is, the society is composed of individuals who see themselves as equal in some more fundamental respect than they are unequal. [MacPherson, 1962]

As we saw earlier, one's status determined the several authorities to whom one was responsible and who had the power to levy fines and corporal punishments. When the state becomes the exclusive agent for the treatment of the defendant, there is an assumption that one's status with regard to the state takes precedence over any other status one might hold. The assumption that impersonal laws of the market and a universal psychology, which coordinated with these laws, provided the conditions wherein such a radical change in notions of political responsibility and obligation became possible.

> So long as everyone was subject to the determination of a competitive
> market, and so long as this apparently equal subordination of individ-
> uals to the determination of the market was accepted as rightful, or
> inevitable, by virtually everybody, there was a sufficient basis for
> rational obligation of all men to a political authority which could
> maintain and enforce the only possible orderly human relations, namely,
> market relations. [MacPherson, 1962, p. 272]

The laws of the market and the principles of an inherent psychology provided the foundation for the separation of law and ethics. And Thomas Hobbes became the first to rationalize this compartmentalization even though at the time the argument was in favor of the monarchy:

> A crime, is a Sinne, consisting in the Committing (by Deed or Word) of that which the Law forbiddeth, or the Omission of what it hath commanded. So that every Crime is a Sinne but not every Sinne a Crime. [Hobbes, 1909, p. 224]

Further, Hobbes argued that crime was the effect of application of a calculable law:

> No Law, made after a fact done, can make it a Crime: because if the Fact be against the Law of Nature, the Law was before the fact; and a Positive Law cannot be taken notice of before it be made and therefor cannot be obligatory. [Hobbes, 1909, p. 226]

The argument then rests on the plausibility of making a significant distinction between the ethics of an act and its legal status. This in turn introduces a distinction between those institutions of authority to which one has a secular obligation and those to which one has a moral obligation. What may have begun as a trial separation ended in a permanent divorce. The divorce was substantially aided by the formalization of legal procedure that was the chief concern of political philosophers of the eighteenth century and the chief *assumption* used by subsequent critics of the prison system. But what must be kept in mind is that these arguments were *themselves* occasioned by a new economic system.

As Weber and others have argued:

> The capitalistic form of industrial organization if it's to operate rationally, must be able to depend upon calculable adjudication and administration . . . the royal 'cheap justice' with its remissions of royal grace introduced continual disturbances into the calculations of economic life. . . . What (capitalism) requires is law which can be counted upon like a machine. [Weber, 1927, p. 343]

Although prison "reformers" turned to Beccaria for enlightenment as to the inequities in the legal system and thus an explanation of the plight of the convict, Becarria himself echoed the needs of a bourgeois society for a kind of law that was as reliable and calculable as those of the market place.

> If the power of interpreting laws be an evil, obscurity in them must be another, as the former is the consequence of the latter. This evil

will be still greater, if the laws be written in a language unknown to the
people; who, being ignorant of the consequences of their own actions,
become necessarily dependent on a few, who are interpreters of the
laws. [Beccaria, 1862, p. 23]

Earlier, Montesquieu had declared that laws, far from being based on divine
revelation of the church, were the formulation of human reason [de Tracy, 1811].
As market place laws were supposedly immune to any particular institution,
human greed or folly and thus equally available for calculations of optimum gain
to all, civil law itself was based on calculability and was said to provide a formula
for measuring proper punishments.

Thus, the efforts of political philosophers were a cause, but more a reflection, of increased rationalization in the economic sphere that found its highest
expression in the law. The modern state was to be a politically based bureaucracy that sought to rationalize the operation of a new type of economic organization. This increasing rationalization of the law was a necessary movement
in making economic decisions and profits predictable—a necessary condition for
the promotion of capitalism. The desire for security and predictability spoke to
the particular needs of an emerging class and were then translated, with the aid
of "reformers," into universal principles of freedom and liberty.

Prison reform, then, in the late eighteenth and early nineteenth centuries
was in fact reform of penal *law*. But, as we shall see, both the establishment of
the penitentiary (the change in substantive practice) and the abolition of
corporate punishment can be seen as a function of the same impetus that
brought success to those earlier "reformers."

Punishment and the Causes of Crime

Penal reformers drew their rhetoric, by and large, from social philosophers
engaged in a parallel but much broader pursuit. The principle of proportion
whereby exact, calculable punishments were afixed to specific offenses was the
product of a campaign that was largely waged to rid the entire society of feudal
elements that impeded the development of a bourgeois political economy. But
problems arose when the ideology of the larger movement was applied to the
specifics of the prison.

Basic to the idea of punishment is the legitimacy of coercion. And coercion
was now to be exercised exclusively by the state. But a state was considered
legitimate only insofar as it guaranteed the widest possible sphere of individual
autonomy. Thus state-imposed incarceration presented at least the appearance
of a contradiction. (For a development of this point, see Murphy [1973].)

There was a very concrete dilemma underlying this problem, for by the
mid-nineteenth century, the antagonism between the state and the bourgeoise

had diminished, although factional disputes continue to this day. It was no longer necessary to protect the bourgeoise as a whole against the arbitrariness of the administration of justice now that the interests of the two had essentially blended. But it was no more in the interests of the liberal state to give up its powers of coercion than it was for the aristocracy preceding it. So if it could not refrain from coercive techniques, some new way to rationalize the activity was required. The practice that failed to fit the theory was countered with a new theory designed to fit the old practice.

An earlier reformer was to presage this contradiction and its reconciliation. For Paley, civil liberty within the new secular state consisted in "not being restrained by any law but what concludes in a greatest degree to the public welfare" [Fletcher, 1939, pp. 195, 197]. Paley's argument and that of other utilitarians rest on the balancing of the inherent evil of incarceration by the social good thereby derived. As Bentham was to argue when militating for the penitentiary he later designed, the only way to justify state coercion is through the social utility provided. The miserable condition of inmates was seen simply as a symptom of the problem—that is, coercion that led to such dreadful effects obviously had little *social* value.

Here the social scientist (or his prototype) was to play a significant helping role. As they pointed out, wrong-doers were victims themselves, either of the environment or of destructive individual characteristics [Radzinowicz, 1966, ch. 2]. Hence, imprisonment, far from restricting an autonomy the individual never enjoyed, would provide the conditions whereby that autonomy would become possible. In the struggle for a more liberal state working within the dictates of the market system, individualism has always been the first line of defense against the encroachment of the traditional aristocracy. This "individual," it was preached

> . . . was free inasmuch as he is proprietor of his person and capacities. . . . Society becomes a lot of free equal individuals related to each other as proprietors of their own capacities and of what they have acquired by their exercise. . . . Political society becomes a calculated device for the protection of this property and for the maintenance of an orderly relation of exchange. [MacPherson, 1962]

Once the modern liberal state was realized, the dilemma became obvious. It was necessary to continue using the assumptions of individualism while exercising the very coercive power such assumptions were originally generated to defeat. The specific way out of the dilemma was to propose that those so coerced were in essence *different* from the self-determining individual for whom the state did exist. And hence penal practices would have to be designed as to make "individuals" out of convicts and thereby increase the public welfare as well.

Besides saving the doctrine of the liberal state from eventual collapse, such ideas served the coincidental purpose of acting as a control on the growing numbers of proletariate—whether they were the immigrants flocking to the "new world" or the "industrial reserve army" of Europe and Great Britain. By the mid-nineteenth century, American penitentiaries were populated by either foreign-born or lower-class unemployed workers. In England between 1805 and 1831, total convictions increased by 54 percent during a period of massive unemployment and poverty.

Once imprisoned, the treatment of the convict would transform him from a remnant of serfdom into a member of the "working" class that both the theory of the liberal state and the practice of capitalism required:

> . . . labor (in penitentiaries) would become not an oppressive task for punishment, but a welcome diversion, a delight rather than a burden. The convict would sit in his cell and work with his tools daily, so that over the course of his sentence regularity and discipline would become habitual. He would return to the community cured of vice and idleness, to take his place as a responsible citizen. [Rothman, 1971, p. 86][e]

The "reform" and "treatment" of prisoners became not only sound doctrine but a good investment.

So the prototypical social scientist was set on his search to hunt for the roots of criminality. The modern penitentiary *does* find its rationale in the "discovery" of the causes of crime, but such "discoveries" are not independent of the claims the modern state must make for the legitimacy of its coercive activities. These claims, as we have seen, originate in the economic and material conditions of the period.

The focus, therefore, of the developing penitentiary was to search the inmates' life histories for explanations of their criminal behavior. In the late eighteenth and nineteenth centuries these explanations were found in either a bad family environment, corrupt relationships, or in particular moral and character-logical weaknesses of the inmate. For example, Rev. J. Clay, writing of the "criminal classes" in mid-nineteenth-century England, presages the "findings" of social science of a century later: "It is the larger town in which disorder and crime are generated" [Tobias, 1967, p. 67].

Data collected on prisoners during the Nineteenth Century in the penitentiaries of the United States indicate the degree of confidence investigators had in the theory of crime that links deviance to a malevolent environment.

---

[e]Rothman is quoting from George W. Smith, "A Defense of the System of Solitary Confinement of Prisoners" (Philadelphia, 1827), p. 24.

The 1829 and 1930 reports of the Auburn penitentiary contained 173
biographies and in fully two-thirds of them, the supervisors selected
and presented data to prove that childhood made the man. [Rothman,
1971, p. 64]

William Channing, first secretary of the New York Prison Association and a
reformer of some note, speaking at the association's first convention in 1844,
voiced the accepted position that was to dictate the treatment of inmates since:

. . . the community is itself, by its neglect and bad usages in part
responsible for the sins of its children. [*Report*, 1844, p. 45]

Channing reasoned, along with hundreds of his contemporary reformers, that by
erecting penitentiaries the community would provide the convict with a new
environment to ameliorate the influences of the old. It would, in addition, pay
off part of the debt that the community "owes the criminal" for its neglect!

If crime was a symptom of personal disease, defect, or maladjustment, it
made good sense to develop penitentiaries suited to the "treatment" of such
problems. That penetentiaries were recommended and existed long before
these "scientific" discoveries, however, could lead one to believe that far from
internment being a practical result of theory, *it was a practice that required a
theory.* Such theories, then, served to both "explain" the disproportionate
numbers of the poor to be found in prison and also to rationalize their sequest-
ered existence.

By the mid-nineteenth century another development occurred that was to
swell the ranks of inmates. This was the general substitution of prison sentences
in most cases for purely corporal punishment. By the nineteenth century, the
idea of convict reform, as we have seen, took its place as the necessary justification of coercive measures. However, if it is claimed that reformation of the
convict—returning him to a state of free individualism—is the only legitimate
function of state coercion, then it would be inconsistent to submit him to public
humiliation or branding—common practices of the era:

To be logical, the law should also declare, that at the expiration of the
punishment the prisoner should receive back his honour and his liberty.
[Beaumont and de Tocqueville, 1833, p. 85]

In so arguing about changes in the French penal code, de Tocqueville lays
bare a very good reason for ridding the penal system of those types of punishments that bring "lasting humiliation." Practices such as branding, banishment,
public whippings, stocks, pillor, and the public cage are totally inconsistent with
a penal ideology that *claims reformation of the convict.* Of course, the abolition

of such treatments speaks more to their *public* quality than to the disgust reformers felt for physical torture. Corporal punishment *continued* to be a treatment of choice long after it ceased to be a public display. In Auburn, the prototype of the new penitentiary, the whip was commonplace. Upon inspecting
the new penitentiaries in 1833, William Crawford was to note:

> Any breach of discipline was forthwith visited by a flogging from the
> wardens, who were all armed with heavy cowhide curring whips; they
> could inflict what amount of stripes they chose only making to the
> superintendent afterwards such reports as they saw fit themselves.
> [*Report on the Penitentiaries of the United States*]

It was not until the twentieth century that corporal punishment in penitentiaries was abolished on any broad scale. For example, the "cat" was retained until 1905 in Maryland's prisons and was only abandoned when physicians
discovered that the blood of victims remaining on the cords of the lash infected
succeeding victims—generally with syphilis.

Obviously each prison reform can be seen as the effect of the effort of
honestly inspired reformers. Nevertheless, no reform is possible on alien soil,
and it was the rich and fertile ideas of the merchantile era that required a different approach to the treatment of transgressors. The commitment to the idea
that incarceration should be the end product of a rational and calculable law;
that it would make a new man out of the faulty material that was the product
of environmental, psychological, or moral defects and that science could lay bare
these causes of crime and thus dictate the structure and operation of the new
penitentiary and end senseless corporal punishment all were necessary to the
consistent operation of the liberal state, which in turn corresponded to the new
economic realities of the period of greatest reform.

Obviously, humanitarian impulses played a large role in changing the structure and functioning of criminal justice system, but we are arguing that humanitarianism was not the exclusive province of any one era. Much earlier, there
were calls for the rejection of harsh treatment of criminals. The question quite
simply is why, at that point in history—the late eighteenth and the nineteenth
centuries—did such pleas not fall on deaf ears? If we are to believe that humanitarian efforts are not inevitably successful, we must somehow account for their
ascendence. Secondly, as Rothman [1971, p. xiv] points out in a slightly different context, once a set of practices are abolished there is a wide variety of
alternative practices only a few of which are seen as viable.

What we have argued is that modern penal practices are the final outcome
of several interwoven factors. First, new theories of political obligation necessitated by changing conditions and social relations bring with them new
theories of the nature of crime. Part of the treatment of crime in the modern
state is an effort to reconcile state coercion with the doctrine of the liberal state

while leaving that doctrine intact. Given this inconsistency, a new theory of the causes and cures of crime must be found in the offender's inherent ability to act as a freely determined member of the society. While he is ultimately responsible for his own behavior and thus a fit candidate for punishment, the state itself cannot be held responsible for coercion, for it is responding to environmental factors and psychological dispositions of the criminal "classes." Far from coercing the convict, punishment would imbue him with capabilities whose absence would lead him back to the same faulty decisions that led to his original criminal behavior. These theories point to a particular class as the "carrier" of crime and explain the disproportionate numbers of those from such classes to be found in prison.

Theory and practice conjoin to both rid society of some of its more barbaric customs and, more importantly and *not* coincidentally, substitute an alternative treatment of problematic members consistent with the terms upon which political power is exercised.

The "Treatment" of the Inmate

It is one very long step from galley slavery, deportation, and penal servitude at hard labor to "a model community in which prisoners will be treated with the most recent developments in behavior modification techniques and which will substitute judicious use of rewards for plain force—as one correctional officer described a new "center" in the planning stages in his state.

The modern prison is no longer a prison but a "center" variously adjectively tagged depending on the preferences of the staff and the "in" jargon of the moment. Patuxent in Maryland is not for punishment of criminals (in fact you can't get there through criminal procedures at all) but for "defective delinquents." No longer are "prisoners" held in Vermont's maximum security institution; only "residents." And no longer does Vermont punish their inmates; they administer doses of "aversion therapy." And when inmates refuse to stay in line, federal grants are procured to allow for the "treatment" of such "deviant offenders."

In California, inmates are "diagnosed." In Florida, the new inmate expecting to see a prison goes instead to a "reception" center, and in New Hampshire they are held in solitary confinement because they are "sick." Yes, there are still "prisons," but they are really relics from another era for the control of those who simply will not or cannot "get better." And these are such a small number that, for example, New England is trying out an idea of using a regional "center" for such trouble makers, leaving the several states free to commit their resources to "treatment."

Of interest to note, however, is that what once were the "criminal classes" now seem to be the "sick classes." For while our social science has turned up new remedies for crime, it has not as yet managed to find a new *class* of criminals. It remains the ever reliable group at the bottom of the economic pyramid.

Conclusions

What we have tried to show is that historical periods characterized by different penal doctrines first display a fundamental change in the notion of political obligation. Medieval institutions were both localistic and universal. Centering on the manor and the church, legal obligation was at best splintered between feudal lords, guilds, and the ecclesiastical court. The means available to guarantee these obligations were reserved by these institutions and were, therefore, differentiated on the basis of the "special status qualities of [their] members" [Weber, 1967, p. 147].

The New Monarchs of the fifteenth and sixteenth centuries claimed a different form of legitimate power based on the support of the middle classes of the town whose interests were served by releasing the powers of a free labor market [de *Jouvenal*, 1949, p. 177].[f] This in turn transformed the notions surrounding law, its enforcement and the doctrines concerning the treatment of criminals.

With the rise of the rational state, the new and powerful entrepreneurial classes were to submit a different kind of political obligation that in turn was based on assumptions regarding the market place and the state's role in the economic sphere of public life. The "modern" penitentiary is understandable as a product of these changes in the economic and political assumptions upon which the liberal state is based.

Two conditions—one political, the other economic—were submitted as the basis of the doctrine of the penitentiary system. One is that it operates within a state that both provides and recognizes full parity of all its members. Secondly, those who fail in these political obligations do so because, independent of the state, they lack the full capability that the doctrine of the state requires of its franchised members. In other words, under these conditions the coercion of citizens is not force but authority. As long as these conditions hold, it was argued, the penitentiary is based on a valid theory of crime and its treatment.

But neither of these conditions do hold. The first fails because a full parity relationship, despite an ideology of universal suffrage, has not been obtained precisely among those groups that make up the largest proportion of the prison population; the second, because it is precisely the policies of the state that produce those conditions that, it is claimed, "cause" crime. Thus the

---

[f]"If the natural tendency of power is to grow, and if it can extend its authority and increase its resources only at the expense of the notables, it follows that its ally for all time is the common people. The passion for absolutism is, inevitably, in conspiracy with the passion for equality."

legitimacy of the prison system is destroyed on its own terms by the political and economic conditions within which it must operate.

The penal dilemma is increasingly clear: the assumptions of nineteenth-century liberalism continue to be used at the very time the structure of the economy cannot provide the material conditions upon which such assumptions are necessarily predicated.

The response of the state to its political dilemma has been to "depoliticalize" the nature of criminal law and the reaction to inmates by the adoption of a medical model of treatment. This effort pervades every aspect of the twentieth-century penitentiary. But, as we will show, it cannot totally obscure the political and economic basis of imprisonment or the inherent contradiction between the prison as an institution of nineteenth-century liberalism operating within twentieth-century corporate capitalism.

2
The Political Economy of Crime

Having traced the development of the modern penal system, we are now in a better position to outline the social doctrine upon which it must rest.

The first foundation entails that the law is equally applied to *all,* that the degree of punishment is calculable with regard to the degree of harm done to the state, and that the law is the sole arbitrator and definer of civilly acceptable behavior.

Secondly, individuals must be claimed to be equally susceptible to the impersonal laws of the market and to the psychological corollaries of these laws. To put a fine point on it, the presupposition is that we are all in the dry goods business; we all know what is expected of us, and we all have equal access to, though not control over, a market that is itself influenced solely by impersonal mechanisms.

The third foundation limits the focus of state coercion; the state may only so act provided that circumstances unrelated to its own actions prevent certain individuals from behaving in a manner commensurate with political equality.

Political obligation—the duty to accept coercion—rests on the applicability of the first two assumptions and implies that one may not be *morally* obliged to accept punishment in their absence. Given the third assumption, political equality and hence obligation rest on key suppositions of the role of the state within the economic sphere. In order to call these assumptions into account, it is necessary to show not only that economic inequality exists, but that it is part of the systemic use of state power and thus undermines the first two assumptions. Secondly, one must show that the conditions that the state claims give rise to crime are, in fact, an *effect* of this economic bias and thus undermine the third assumption.

Insofar as these conditions do *not* obtain, it becomes necessary to either radically alter the role of the state or to radically alter conceptions of what criminality *is*—thereby obscuring the political nature of crime. The current method employed in this quest has been to depoliticize the definition of crime. Criminals are to be viewed as "anti-social psychopaths" needing forcible "treatment." Thus, state-supported social inequities that violate the conditions of political obligation can be shrouded in a fog of medical and technical verbiage.

The ideology underlying our current penal and educational systems took root in a very different economic setting. The entrepreneurial system that replaced feudalism was marked by the need for a rational but *limited* state, as the entrepreneurs could count on their own abilities, expanding markets, and a readily available, "liberated" work force. Material conditions, however, have changed decidedly, and the "free" market has been replaced with some variant of state capitalism. As outlets dried up and unhampered competition threatened to ravage the delicate structure upon which the economy was based [Baran and Sweezy, 1966; Kolko, 1963], the government increasingly became an economic provider and absorber.

> One out of twenty-four workers was on some government payroll in 1900; the proportion rose to one out of fifteen in 1920, one out of eleven in 1940, one out of eight in 1949. In 1920, one out of every fourteen dollars of capital assets (excluding military equipment) was government property; in 1946 the proportion became one out of four. [Burns, 1954, p. 46]

> Whereas in 1929 less than one dollar in ten of national production owed its origin to government purchasing, today about one dollar in five of all goods and services produced is sold to some branch of government. [Heilbroner, 1962, p. 175]

Our question is, on whose behalf did and does the government act? Our claim is that far from intruding on the perogatives of the wealthy, the state has played a mediating role, the ultimate purpose of which was to maintain the economic privileges of a relative few. The increasing encroachment of the government in a traditionally *laissez-faire* economy has brought with it the rhetoric of universal education, universal employment, and guarantees of equal justice for all. The fact that the government is taking the role of protector of these rights is significant in itself. Of more significance is *how* that power has been used. We will begin with the results of a half-century-old "graduated" income tax—a direct governmental measure ostensibly designed to ensure fiscal freedom for those at and near the bottom of the economic ladder.

The top 1 percent of our population holds over 20 percent of all personal wealth, while the bottom 20 percent only accounts for little over 5 percent. The top 5 percent holds more wealth than the entire bottom 40 percent [Upton and Lyons, 1970]. There is hardly a zealot alive so deadened to reality as to claim that such massive disproportions are an accidental rather than central part of the fiscal functioning of the state. We will now examine the educational and vocational structures to see how this disparity is worked out and maintained.

It is a truism that the educational system reflects the national class structure at the lower levels of schooling. There is no shortage of material on the failures of those understaffed institutions. What is also true is that secondary education mirrors this original screening process. Those attending traditional four-year colleges, for example, are twice as likely to come from families with incomes exceeding $15,000 as those attending more explicitly vocational colleges. Many college students from lower-income families have to support themselves by part-time work or have to drop out entirely to support their families.

These factors are reflected in the fact that college men whose fathers had completed college are over six times as likely to complete college as those whose father had not completed eight grades of schooling [Greer, 1970, p. 560]. We will now demonstrate how state policies play an active role in perpetuating these educational inequalities.

The economic expansion of the 1950s and early 1960s allowed and necessitated unprecedented expenditures on higher education. The early 1970s, however, brought two subsequent dilemmas. First, the economy was in need of cooling off, and second, the state was creating too many "overeducated" workers. Our technocracy *does* need a literate work force, but not as many as were being produced. Hence, those federal and corporate funds were cut back as dramatically as they had been augmented; tuitions were raised and scholarships, along with teaching jobs, were cut back. The higher educational and thus vocational tracks were made even more inaccessible to those from the wrong side of the tracks.

The results has been a *deliberately* created surplus of teachers, scientists, and engineers coupled with a decrease of "interest" in liberal arts colleges. In 1970, for example, 17 percent of Chicago's junior college students were in vocational/technical programs. That percentage is now being raised to 60 percent [Rothstein, 1971]. As a Gillette personnel man said, "If you take a controller and put him into a menial bookkeeping job, how long will it be before his ego will cause a clash with the middle managers above him?"[a] The solution, of course, is not to upgrade jobs and responsibility or to share them among various workers thus doing away with these "ego clashes," but to nip the problem in the bud—that is, to limit the number of "vocational egos."

The best way to do this is to perpetually upgrade the degree of *certification* required for all jobs. Studies have shown that among paper technicians, bank tellers, secretaries, textile workers, utility installers, auto workers, insurance agents, electrical engineers, and scientists, there was *no* correlation between job performance and level of formal education. Further,

Air traffic personnel working at the Federal Aviation Agency [need] the characteristics that technical college training might be expected to develop . . . yet half of the 507 air controllers who had attended government rating 14 or above had no formal schooling beyond high school.

Further, there was no pattern of differences in job grades among men with different school records. . . . *Nevertheless, F.A.A. Officials expect to raise the schooling requirements for new employees in the future.* [New University Conference, 1971, p. 2; italics added]

---

[a]"Employers Shun Job-Seekers Who Are Overqualified for Job Openings," *The Wall Street Journal*, December 29, 1970.

In 1910, only about one of eight adults had gone beyond high school, yet one in three held white-collar jobs and many others had technical jobs. All such vocations today require at least a high school diploma. But given the treadmill effect inherent in a competitive society, such jobs are not easier to come by; they simply require more *expensive* training [Berg, 1970].

It is fashionable in some quarters to claim that population declines are responsible for recent declines in educational outlays. But the simple fact is that classes are more overcrowded today than they were during the height of federal spending on education. People would obviously *like* to go to college. State fiscal policies, however, are making that nearly impossible for many. It seems clearly more fruitful to examine the shifting needs of those controlling the political economy than to mull over charts of birth and death rates to explain social change. Regardless of projected population changes, it is nearly inevitable that we will soon experience a "glut" of computer programmers, as the system continues its elusive, discriminatory dance.

The 1973 Carnegie Commission on Education estimates that in this decade some 3 million Americans will receive educational certificates which will *not* lead them to any job even vaguely requiring such training. And hard as it will be for those with advanced degrees to get work, those placed in the non-degree categories, except for those seeking menial labor, will, predictably, be in deep trouble.

The basis of that dismal predictability concerns the other area of state-maintained inequality mentioned at the outset—jobs in general, unemployment in specific—for the educational and vocational structures interface within the confines of the economic system. And the relevant constraint is the perpetual drive for some level of unemployment. It is rather apparent that it is in the rational, calculating interests of those with power to perpetuate some degree of vocational instability in *others.*

Note, for example, that the 1945 *Full* Employment Bill was altered to include only the goal of "*maximum* employment . . . in a manner calculated to foster and promote free competitive enterprise . . .". Full employment has become Newspeak for at least 4 percent of the *counted* work force being out of work. There may be yearly fluctuations as government spending, inflationary, or recessionary pressures and tax policies respond to variables, but at bottom there will be a fairly sizable number of souls unsuccessfully seeking work.

This precarious situation functions to keep wages and all union demands within safe boundaries by dangling the threat of imminent replacement over the heads of those with marginal jobs. (And that, it turns out, includes more of us than we had previously thought.) It also serves to cool off an inflation-prone economic system by reducing total demand for goods, thus holding a lid of sorts on prices. The 1973 H.E.W. *Task Force on Work in America* stated that there are between 10 and 30 million Americans who would work if jobs were available. In March 1973, a White House spokesman said that, although unemployment was up, the absolute number of jobs had been increasing. This, he stated, was proof that the economy was "healthy."

The examples we have been displaying should reveal the obvious implausibility in holding to the critical presumption that we are all equally susceptible to *impersonal* laws of the market place—that is, we are *not* all in the dry goods business, at least we do not all *own* the stores. Some of us work for those who own the "stores," and drastic income differentials and vocational instability are simply not unrelated to the functioning of the state. Far from finding himself in the midst of an impersonal, egalitarian market place, the average citizen is thrown into a tightly controlled political and economic arrangement in which the power of the wealthy is variously protected by the state. At the time of the White House spokesman's statement about rising unemployment in a "healthy" economy, the economy *was* healthy. And that is precisely our point.

Reform and Individuation

As Rothman [1971, ch. II] points out, the nineteenth century's diagnosis of the causes of crime in a poor social environment both distinguished it from earlier conceptions and laid the groundwork for a new penitentiary system that was to rehabilitate both the inmate and society. Since that time, schooling as well as prisons have been conceived as instruments of social change. The great appeal of social reform through specific institutions was that all issues of distributive social justice were translated into notions of individual ability and effort in school and market place.

The underlying assumption of modern education is that social reform is attainable largely through individual effort—with relatively minimal and painless social changes. Those theories of educational betterment *that have been acted on* are invariably couched in the rhetoric of increasing *individual* ability. But by ignoring the social considerations intimately involved in the initial problem, this approach is generally rendered worthless. *Ensuing failures are then used to justify total neglect in other areas of social deprivation.* The form this is taking today with regard to the failure of the educational system is to trot out theories about racial inferiority that have been functionally dormant since the last world war. What is of note is not that individuals persist in such empty, demented work, but its current reception as gospel in academic, governmental, and other circles.

One such theorist puts the greatest thinkers of the modern era to shame with brilliant insights such as, "The morality of lower-class culture is preconventional, which means that the individual's actions are influenced not by conscience but only by a sense of what he can get away with." He adds, "It is to be expected, then, that when male adolescence and lower-class culture meet in the same person they will interact, reinforce each other, and produce an extraordinary high propensity toward crime." A final touch is in order: "Young people as such differ from the lower class as such in at least one very important respect; they dislike hurting people. When they employ violence, it is as a means rather than as an end in itself" [Banfield, 1968, pp. 163, 168, 169].

In order to comprehend and "justify" such failures as perpetual unemployment, the tens of millions of Americans who cannot even read, and so forth, one must, at some point, make a basic choice: One must either seek explanations in the various institutional functions surrounding such failures, with profound political implications, or one must *depoliticalize* such activities. One may then rely on a purely individualized approach covered with a variety of obscuring theories and backed up with heavy doses of the most modern technology available. Hence, we have the advent of complex-teaching-modular-systems, theories of racial inferiority and drugging of unruly elementary students in inner city schools, and the daily television star warning us of the difficulties in getting work if we drop out of school.

We are now ready for the final link in this phase of our argument. And that is the claim that the people who are bounced in and out of school and in and out of work are the exact same class of people who are bounced in and out of jail. And that this is no accident.

Given as we are to the ideology of individualism, a natural tendency is to view the average inmate as a less than bright individual who is having intellectual difficulties in coping with a technological society. In fact, studies show that the average intelligence of inmates is equal to if not superior to the national norm. Their *reading* levels, however, are between the seventh and eighth grade levels [Bagdikian and Dash, 1972, p. 134; Barnes and Tetters, 1959, p. 7]. What this indicates is that those who have been pushed off the vocational/educational ladder tend disproportionately to end up in jail—that is, the exact same screening process at work in the "outside" world is brought to play in deciding what is defined as criminal and who must be punished. This is not to deny that the poor do commit a disproportionate amount of a *kind* of crime and receive a disproportionate amount of a *kind* of punishment—both highly visible. What distinguishes the poor from the wealthy is not the *amount* of wrong doing but its visibility and the amount of attention it is given by the state.

As we discussed in our opening chapter, notions of criminality fluctuate over time, the only constant in the Western World being the *class* from which those deemed criminal will be effectively chosen. And that is the class which, as we have shown, is effectively prevented from enjoying the full fruits of our society. In brief, the presumption of equal access to the market place is denied and denied by actions of the state. What must now be shown is how the state operates with regard to the second presumption necessary to justify the penitentiary; how the state systematically discriminates against a particular class of people with regard to criminal justice, how that discrimination generally precludes the notion of political obligation, and how the state's awareness of this leads to a variety of obscuring or repressive reactions.

Who Goes There?

Our penal system is nothing if it is not selective of whom it will admit under its care. Something like a fraction of 1 percent of all actual crime ends up with the offender serving time, so there is ample opportunity to screen out those deemed too undesirable to enter the system. So the poor are blessed again. Eighty percent of the million-plus Americans doing this come from the bottom 12 percent of wealth holders. Rothman reports that the contemporary economic makeup of our prison population has not changed significantly from what was the case a century ago:

> The annual reports of the state penitentiaries made eminently clear that the overwhelming majority of inmates stood toward the bottom of the social ladder . . . in almost every state prison, laborers and semi-skilled workers filled the rolls. . . . The total number of professionals, merchants, shopkeepers and farmers, in a sample of some eighteen hundred convicts in 1849 was less than three percent. [Rothman, 1971, p. 253]

The natural response to this in our society is to blame the victim. Poor people, it is reasoned, *do* commit more crime. Slums breed that sort of thing, but

> All social classes commit significant amounts of crime. In 1947, James Wellenstein and Clemet J. Wylie listed 49 serious crimes with a minimum sentence of two years; of 1,698 responses from a cross-section of New York inhabitants weighted toward the more affluent, 91 percent admitted to one or more crimes without ever being arrested.

> Austin Potterfield compared criminal offenses of college students with 2,000 boys who had been sent to juvenile court; 100 percent of male and female students had committed at least one of the offenses for which the 2,000 other boys had been sent to court. [Bagdikian and Dash, 1972, p. 154]

Bill Haney, Martin Gold, Jay Williams and Myrtle Blum conducted a survey in the 1960s of 1,369 juvenile delinquents and stated, "We found no strong relationship between social status and delinquent behavior" [Haney and Gold, 1973]. According to Professor Lemert, "It has been estimated that the 'average' law-abiding citizen in one day unwittingly commits enough crime to call for five years of imprisonment and fines running close to three thousand dollars" [Lemert, 1951, p. 317, in Szasz, 1963, p. 106].

In brief, the notion that the lower classes are more criminal (with its smug implications of superiority for those not in those classes) is simply false. But the *functional* definition of crime is behavior for which people pay with their freedom. And all that means is illegal behavior of the poor, the near poor, and the non-white. In order for this to be the case, however, the state necessarily violates its putative role as neutral mediator of civil and criminal harms. This violation has been systematically achieved by the selectiveness used to punish illegal behavior and through the mechanisms made available to avoid that punishment.

The law, in its infinite impartiality and blindness, presumes innocence. But bail, for those who can't raise it, convicts as surely as a trial. One inmate put it this way:

> You are guilty of the crime of poverty, a crime punishable by indefinite incarceration, loss of income, irreparable damage to your reputation, and as often as not the loss of friends and family. . . .
> No ambition or initiative and no faith in the *free* enterprise system. Your empty pockets are damning evidence of your general untrustworthiness and probable guilt.

> [In jail awaiting trial in lieu of bail] you will be kept so goddamned "safe" that you will feel buried. By this time, of course, the question of your guilt or innocence is irrelevant since the cumulative effects of long imprisonment, loss of contacts and suppressed rage and frustration have caused you to cop a plea, go insane or add new charges to those already pending. [*Luparar,* Vermont State's Prisoner Newsletter, November 1972, p. 21–22]

What must be noted is that those "others" are often not just *temporarily* let free. A Rand Institute study of the New York judicial process clearly demonstrated that *in comparable cases,* men out on bail before a trial are less often found guilty when the trial comes up [Bagdikian and Dash, 1972]. Over half of our jail population are people who have not yet come to trial!

The normal minimum fee for a trial lawyer in a Superior Court runs around $500, plus another $500 per appeal, plus all investigative costs.[b] The good firms, of course, charge much more. Yet fully one-third of American families have no savings account at all; the median holding for those who do is $1,300 [*St. Louis Post Dispatch,* Dec. 3, 1971] ; and half of our population is in debt.

But, it is said, no one goes without legal counsel. The state has attempted to equalize a poor man's splended chance through the mechanism of the court-appointed lawyer. As in so many other areas of reform, however, there is less here than meets the eye and more involved that the overall fact that the state spends over four times as much on prosecution as it does on indigent defense [Bureau of the Census, Chart No. 244, 1972]. As disproportionate as these

---

[b]This estimation was provided by the New Hampshire Legal Aid Services through a private communication from Richard Cotten, an attorney for that agency.

figures are, they do not tell the full story. It seems quite clear that court-appointed lawyers are not only disinclined to extend themselves on their cases, they are very much inclined to "*lose*" them! To better understand this claim, it is necessary to remember that, like educational, vocational, and tax benefits, legal assistance is distributed on a scarce-resource basis—that is, on the basis of ability to pay (or avoid payment). The motivation for those lawyers who do not go into private practice, excluding the idealistic or incompetent, is political advancement and/or job security. They make less money working for the government. As one inmate told us, "Without those court-appointed cases, many lawyers would starve." The point, though, is that their "starvation" depends on their being *given* cases, not on their *winning* them. The result of this structurally induced imperative is that a defendant represented by a court-appointed attorney is significantly more likely to plea bargain. In New Hampshire, for example, almost 70 percent of the inmates in the maximum security prison were represented by court-appointed attorneys; 57 percent of these had pled guilty to lesser charges—"coping a plea." As the figures in Tables 2-1 and 2-2 show and as these inmates clearly knew, so pleading pays off in the long run by a shorter sentence. What it does *not* provide is the possibility that the defendant will go free.

Ninety percent of criminal cases involve coping a plea. Justice Warren Burger has stated that if this figure were lowered by just 10 percent, it would require an immediate doubling of judicial manpower and throw the system into chaos. One of the most-persistent complaints we heard from inmates concerned the quality of justice they had received. Many were more upset about their treatment in court than in prison! The Public Defender System, a decent sounding method of "equalizing" economic and hence judicial inequities, is no different from so many other reforms within the context of an economically skewed, competitive society. It doesn't approach its own stated goals. As another inmate writes in the court-barred prison newsletter:

The new "System" does away with such things as Pretrial discovery work for the defendant, not that there ever was much done anyway. . . . If an accused demands his rights to Jury Trial, he is guaranteed a heavy sentence. The question of *acquittal* never enters the picture. After all, too many acquittals would mean no Judgeship, and oh my God! we couldn't have that. The Vermont District Court of Star Chamber will now become the meat market that it was originally intended to be. . . .

This system is ideal for lawyers. The rich are protected anyway, and the lawyers can't make any MONEY from the poor, so who cares about them? Thus far the "Defenders" have delivered *one-hundred percent convictions.* [*Luparar,* Oct. 1972, p. 13]

Table 2-1
Relationship between Types of Pleas and Imprisonment

Plea	Percent imprisoned	Percent receiving over one year sentence
Not guilty, changed to guilty	38.3	26.7
Guilty	43.4	31.7
Found guilty by court	53.3	40.4
Found guilty by jury	72.2	57.6

Source: *Federal Offenders in the United States District Courts, 1965.* Administrative Office of the U.S. Courts.

Table 2-2
Average Sentences Imposed by 88 U.S. District Courts, 1965 (in years)

Guilty plea at arraignment	5.0
Not guilty changed to guilty	5.6
Convicted by court	6.5
Convicted by jury	11.4

Source: *Federal Offenders in the United States District Courts, 1965.* Administrative Office of the U.S. Courts.

Figures are readily available to demonstrate the inherent class bias in current sentencing procedures—the heart of the social definition of crime. In Table 2-3, compare, for example, judicial reactions to auto theft, robbery, larceny/theft on one hand versus fraud and embezzlement on the other. The former category is more likely to be committed by the poor and near poor, whose contact with wealth is more visual than proximate.

Fully 20 percent of all crimes falling in the larceny/theft category are for bicycle theft! A Presidential Commission has estimated annual losses at more than $1.5 billion for fraud and embezzlement, or five times as much as is lost in conventional robberies [*U.S. News and World Report,* Mar. 12, 1973]. This, of course, does not count "normal" overcharging which, for example, has been estimated to run into billions of dollars from privately owned utility companies alone [Metcalf and Reinemer, 1967]. In all federal courts in 1971, 71 percent of those convicted of auto theft received an average sentence of three years,

Table 2-3
Relationship between Types of Criminal Charges and Treatment Received

	Convicted	Imprisoned	Probation	Fined
Larceny/theft	3,320	1,472	1,772	76
Auto theft	2,418	1,715	693	10
Robbery	1,359	1,249	110	none
Embezzlement/fraud	3,824	1,107	2,480	237

Source: *Statistical Abstract of the United States, 1972,* Chart No. 242.

while at the same time 16.3 percent of those convicted of securities fraud were given an average term of 1.7 years [Seymour, 1973, p. 58].

Elevator safety, work safety, mining conditions, and farm laborer conditions are among the many areas receiving daily publicity concerning violent deaths resulting from corporate calculations of profitability versus the cost of safety. But inevitably, those responsible, if ever caught, are given symbolic fines or small sentences in minimum security prisons. In much the same way that our society tends to look down upon any form of manual labor, if such labor is employed in illegally transfering money, the offender stands a greater chance of losing his freedom than if more indirect—though often far more violent—means are employed. This mentality is captured in a fanciful way by Bruce Jay Friedman in his novel *The Dick.*

> "You know who I hate," said the cop. "I don't hate Eichmann. Oh no, not really. And I don't hate Hitler either. Not down deep. You know who I hate?"
>
> "Who's that?"
>
> "Anyone who does crime in the streets."
>
> "It's getting to be quite a problem," said LePeters. [Friedman, 1971, p. 51]

The notion of calculating inherent harm to the society is systematically violated or just ignored in our judicial process. Thus, another link of the chain of justifications for the penitentiary system is undercut. That poor people tend to do less damage to the society is not testimony to their "inherent" goodness. It simply speaks to the obvious fact that they are not in a position to do that harm. Only the wealthy are, and the damage they continue to do is nothing short of staggering. Yet they end up appointing, not petitioning, wardens. Our class bias in the sentencing of offenders represents a full-circle reversion to the medieval notion of tying one's class status to one's punishment. Only today we cannot admit it since our notions of state authority and its concomitant, political obligation rest on the presumption that the state in its coercive activities recognizes no class distinctions.

Within the circle of class discrimination lie both racial and sexual discrimination that, in exaggerated form, support our thesis of the incompatibility of the rationales used to justify the penitentiary and the actual practices therein.

Almost half of our nation's prison population is non-white, over half of those legally executed since 1930 and half of those killed by policemen on the street are black. Blacks represent a significant section of the lower class in this country, and we have shown that the poor in general do not exhibit disproportionate overall criminal tendencies. The same can be said of blacks in specific comparison to whites. The reason we associate blacks with crime is simply that they are treated *by the state* differently than whites.

In Florida, a judge may place a label of "guilty" on a person's probation record or simply leave it off. An analysis of almost 2,500 such cases was made, and *in similar cases* from 40 to 60 percent *more* blacks were sent out with that stigma. Between 1940 and 1965, in the same state, 133 white men and 150 black men were found guilty of rape. Fewer than 5 percent of the whites received the death penalty while over a third of the blacks were executed [Bagdikian, 1972, p. 156].

Furthermore, non-whites on the whole serve more real time in prison than their white counterparts [Federal Bureau of Prisons, 1970]. In those five states that rank highest in actual length of sentence served, 45 percent of the inmate population is black. In the five jurisdictions ranking lowest on this scale, only 17 percent are so colored. It may be argued that the disparity results from the kind of crime non-whites commit as compared to whites. But in the prisons that keep their inmates the longest assault accounts for 10 percent of all convictions, and in the prisons that keep inmates the shortest time the percentage was 9 percent—just 1 percent lower. Sentences for tax evasion for whites average 12.8 months. For blacks it is 28.6 months [*The New York Times,* Sept. 1972]. Overall, however, average *sentences* for non-whites are lower than those for whites (61.6 versus 63.0 months). But, most damning of all, the actual time *served* is higher for the former than the latter, as they serve a greater percentage of their original sentence [Federal Bureau of Prisons, 1970]. (Unfortunately, it is only by extrapolating that we can make this comparison since the publication does not directly tabulate time served and race, but only sentence length and race.)

While the problems of women are certainly not all economic, the class bias does *not* discriminate on the basis of sex. Half of all inmates at women's prisons earned under $3,000 the year before they entered jail. When those in poverty or need are forced into a job like prostitution, they are treated by the state as immoral—not as victims. And so we find that in 1968 the District of Columbia prosecuted 112 men for patronage of prostitutes, while 8,000 women were prosecuted for being on the short end of the stick [Bagdikian, 1972, pp. 82–83].

The state, then, is clearly responsible for inequitable treatment in determining loss of freedom. It is similarly deficient in its role of *freeing* those it has imprisoned.

In spite of the fact that the cost of keeping an adult under parole or probation supervision is significantly lower than that of keeping him in a state penal institution, despite the vastly improved recidivism rates for those under such supervision, and despite the fact that two-thirds of all offenders are under probation or parole supervision, those services receive less than one-third of monies allocated for correctional purposes. Ninety-six percent of our probation officers have caseloads exceeding 40 people, and of the 250 counties surveyed by the President's Commission on Law Enforcement and the Administration of Justice, fully one-third had no probation services at all [Chamber of Commerce, 1972]. As is true of the court-appointed lawyer, statistical disproportions, while revealing, do not tell the full story. The dedication of these state employees is questionable.

The case of Mr. N. is instructive. This man had spent some years in various penitentiaries throughout the country. He had served his time in the Vermont State Prison with a minimum of disciplinary problems and was looking forward to getting out, getting a job, and living with a girl friend who had moved up from the South to stay with him. On April 12, 1973, he was given a full parole contingent only upon his obtaining work. But when you consider that he would have been happy pumping gas, finding work proved to be surprisingly difficult.

Part of his difficulty lay in the fact that the prison would not release any "correctional" guards to take him job hunting. His probation officer kept a similar distance. Day after day went by, appointment after appointment was broken until the officer finally wrote the inmate a letter in which he explained his delay:

> I have been extremely busy with other aspects of my job. On Tuesday I had to attend a meeting of all parole officers in the state. Wednesdays are out of the question, as I have conferences all day; the past two Thursdays were taken up with unexpected problems that arose in the office. As you know, Friday was Good Friday, and so was only a half day. . . . I have had to spend much time in Burlington and Rutland so I have not had time to attend to your problems. . . . I notice that you could not find work in the two places you mentioned to me in our last

meeting, so I suppose this eliminates all the persons, places and things you might look forward to in the way of work.[c]

Mr. N. had to somehow get that parole officer to take him around for job interviews, and he then was given just one day's journey to find a job. After a month of inaction on the part of the officer, we made some pointed inquiries to his superiors and received the assurance that Mr. N. was a "difficult case" but that all was being taken care of. By the middle of June, he was released from prison and rejoined society. During his last month and a half behind bars, he had lived with the constantly thwarted hope that someone would take him around for jobs. He had clipped out want ads offering the sort of work he sought and watched as those ads disappeared. He was extremely agitated when we saw him (informally, at the request of an inmate friend) and had begun to get into fights. If the parole officer's neglect had continued, it seems reasonable to suppose that Mr. N. would have become enough of a "management problem" that his parole would have been indefinitely lifted.

In order to prevent the abuse of having the prison "forget" that an individual is in their custody, in Vermont the prison is required to grant inmates either a parole hearing, at which the inmate is present, or a parole review, at which he need not be, every six months. We interviewed about half of the 30 men who were coming up for one such review and found that only 6 of them knew it was happening! Of those who did know, *none* had been told by their parole officer; they had found out by overhearing guards or other prison officials or by asking their more learned inmate friends. Most of those we spoke to didn't even know the difference between a hearing and a review.

Once out on parole, convicts are kept on exceedingly tight reins. Parole violations range from the commission of further crimes to drinking, from meeting with people the board deems unfit to motor vehicle violations. All of the inmates we saw had roots in relatively small towns where they were highly visible targets for harassment. A very common fear among inmates was the fear of going home to their local police, and we not uncommonly heard parole boards cautioning inmates about this situation. The inmates we saw were generally more frightened of their own police than of making bad personal contacts or life choices once released.

The use to which such police power is put and the acquiesence of the parole boards is revealed in the following, stark simple fact: fully two out of three ex-convicts on parole who are forcibly returned to jail are recommitted on the basis of *parole* violations—*not* because of actions that normally involve police action [Chamber of Commerce, 1972].

---

[c]The inmate in question showed us this letter from his parole officer. For obvious reasons we cannot reveal the name of the recipient.

Of course the ostensive reason for incarceration is to recreate the offender—that is, to make him an educated, productive member of the just society that he has wronged. In some cases, vocational training can be rather successful.

> 1964 U.S. Department of Labor Manpower Administration experience showed that when ex-offenders are placed in appropriate jobs, their rate of recidivism is two to three times less than that of ex-offenders who do not receive job assistance; and ex-offenders with better paying jobs are much less likely to be recidivists than those with no jobs, part-time jobs and lower-paying jobs. [Chamber of Commerce, 1972]

But to talk about vocational rehabilitation for *all* inmates in the face of a job shortage outside of jail is to talk in riddles. What are they being trained for? At two maximum security prisons we investigated, vocational rehabilitation was one of the lasting sources of bitter humor on the part of staff and inmate alike. For the most part, the work given inmates is of the bus-boy, janitor variety or involves the production of a simple item manufactured nowhere else in the country—license plates.

In one of the disciplinary hearings we attended, an inmate from a particularly poor family was been admonished for refusing to attend a car mechanic training program. The reason was simply that it would have taken him away from his regular prison job for half a day. He couldn't afford to lose that income (the inmates had just received a raise to .33¢ per hour). He was, of course, found guilty and is now officially on his way to becoming an incorrigible hardcore who refuses all help.

Since the bulk of inmates have had little effective formal education, the penitentiary has established educational programs. Fiscal priorities in this area are interesting. While the federal government in 1972 spent over half a billion dollars on "protection of federal systems" and "assistance to state and local police" (meaning hardware of various sorts and obvious ends), only $8.8 million was spent on inmate education [Bureau of the Census, 1972, chart no. 245]. Financing of state institutions on the local level reveals identical tendencies. In New Hampshire, Governor Meldrim Thompson's inaugural speech called for "law and order" as well as a reorientation of the State Crime Commission from rehabilitation back to crime prevention: "The threat of disturbances in our penal institutions should not deter us from our responsibilities to protect all the citizens from violence." However, he cut many items from the prison budget and warned the legislature that he would not engage in a "spending spree."

The following March, a near "riot" was followed by a general prison lock-up. Whether the "riot" was a reality or manufactured by the custodial staff is unclear. One correctional officer claimed that it

> was imposed . . . because of dissatisfaction among guards rather than
> trouble from inmates. [*Concord Monitor,* April 24, 1973]

One week after the lock-up, fiscal reverberations were felt. As the local news-
paper reports:

> Warden Joseph C. Vitek asked the [House Appropriations Committee]
> to reinstate several items cut from his original budget by Governor
> Thompson. He also sought additional funds—including $35,000 for
> telephones and radios, $100,000 for transfer of troublesome prisoners
> and seven new staff positions.

> The warden asked the committee to reconsider the $30,000 he put in
> his original request to pay the salaries of five additional correctional
> officers. "We're drastically understaffed in the field of security at the
> institution," Vitek said. [*Concord Monitor,* March 14, 1973]

One member of the "drastically understaffed" custodians, however, was
cooling his heels in the prison's hospital ward. And, by chance, that was the very
same guard who publicly claimed that the whole lock-up was instigated by the
behavior of the guards, not the inmates:

> I must be there [in the hospital wing] as an extra. There's no need
> for me there. They just don't want me in the cell block. [*Concord
> Monitor,* April 25, 1973]

In January 1974, the New Hampshire Crime Commission was faced with a
$36,331 grant to be taken from existing L.E.A.A. funds. Its purpose would be
to appoint a full time lawyer to represent all prisoners. (The lawyer would be
barred from suing the prison.) The Commission turned down the request on the
grounds that "it was too expensive" [*Valley News,* January 21, 1974].

The state *has* recognized that social inequities exist but its efforts at artificially eliminating those inequities—through court-appointed lawyers, prison-
appointed lawyers, and the like—are constrained by the more pervasive dictates
of the political economy's need for vocational and educational instability among
the poor and near poor. The state has systematically excluded people from
certain groups and subgroups and has systematically included those very same
people in its penal system. Such reforms as have in fact been made have come
in response to political pressure, which in turn emanated from the horror at the
conditions of the oppressed. But such reforms are necessarily limited by the
constraints of the political economy and are, in any case, crippled by their
individualistic orientation. Yet expectations have risen as many in general and
prisoners in particular have begun increasingly militant movements on their own

behalf. Again, the system as a whole is confronted with a basic choice: to accede to the radical demands or to obscure, individualize, and technologize the problem.

> Thus, in April 1970, President Nixon sent to the Department of H.E.W. a recommendation of his personal physician that all children be tested at age six to identify criminal potential; and that the potential criminals be "treated" by being placed in state-run camps.[d]

> And in the same month, the Commissioner of Education, Dr. James Allen, proposed that all American children should be "diagnosed" at age two and a half for "home and family background, cultural and language deficiencies, health and nutritional needs, and general potential as an individual." This information would then be computerized and sent to a team of trained professionals whose job it would be to write a detailed prescription for the child and, if necessary, for his home and family as well. [Rothstein, 1971, p. 16]

This sophisticated form of brute force, smacking as it does of totalitarianism, represents the ultimate in personalizing a problem while institutionalizing the solution. Instead of focusing attention on the *institutional* failures of various reforms, the ideology behind such practices allows us to simply blame the victim, "explain" his deviancy, and form policy accordingly. We see this codified in both, not coincidentally, schools and jails through the rapid increase of sanctioned drugging as a method of control. Over one-quarter of the inmates at the Vermont State Prison are administered tranquilizing drugs of one sort or another. Nurses at the New Hampshire State Prison have told us that more librium than aspirin is administered. We asked one warden about the voluntary–involuntary nature of such drug taking. He responded:

> At first, most of them refuse. But we checked with the state's attorney, and if we make a call to the doctor and if we decide that the inmate is an immediate security risk, we can administer the drugs against the inmate's will, if necessary. In some cases we had to strap the man down, but after they are forced to take them, most of the guys here got the message and don't resist.

The significance of drug usage lies not in an occasional quelling of an unruly inmate through his veins, but in the day-to-day use of such deadening chemicals. This represents the highest—or lowest—form of social control and is a tacit

---

[d]Nixon's physician, Dr. Hutschnecker, said that his program would be a "direct, immediate effective way of attacking the problem at its very origin, by focusing on the criminal mind of the child" [Mitford, 1973, p. 56].

admission by those in power than in deep respects their power is tenuous. While the more articulate and political inmates are aware of all this, there is presently little they can do except to point out the results and salvage what little humor remains.

> You can crawl under your bed and hope for the best or let them dope
> you up and turn you into a vegetable. If you're lucky, you'll turn
> into a carrot and can spend all that mindless time playing with that
> pretty green tassel growing out of your head. [*Luparar,* December,
> 1972, p. 6]

Conclusion

In devising the liberal state, new doctrines of political obligation had to be formed. These, in turn, rested on assumptions about social and economic conditions in the absence of which obligation to the state could not be said to exist.

In asserting its right to punish transgressors, the state must either tacitly insist that these conditions do hold or that it is not punishing failure of civil obligation but in fact treating the failures of a *person.*

The economic distribution of resources and politically allocated institutional needs have in fact acted contrary to the egalitarian ideas of the liberal state. These in turn have produced conditions that seemingly are responsible for the greatest number of law breakers. Far from the state recognizing its own responsibility for these conditions, they are perpetuated while the state presumes to attend to the "victims."

Compounding this is the fact that the state through systematic and planful practices places its strongest constraint—imprisonment—against the non-white poor even though the greatest social costs of crime can be laid to the activities of the white non-poor.

Since, to act contrary to the political doctrine of liberalism would seriously jeopardize the actual practices of the state (corporate capitalism [Kolko, 1963]), the state has perpetuated a doctrine of punishment that masks the political aspects of crime by calling it "illness." The fact remains that there is a serious discontinuity between what the state claims for itself and what it actually does. The result of the discontinuity is to indulge in coercive activities for which there is no *political* justification or remedy.

In the following chapters we will examine the organizational, interpersonal, and conceptual binds in which the prison—incapable of acting in accordance with its own prerequisites— must place the inmate.

3

The Self and Its Enemies

In proportion to the degree that political obligation is invalidated by state actions inconsistent with that doctrine, the one institution empowered to punish crimes against the state—the "people's surrogate"—must necessarily reassert the validity of that doctrine for these transgressors. But in the absence of social conditions that could render it a sensible theory of civil responsibility, the use of political doctrine can become treacherous. Such practices make a mockery of political life outside the prison and produce psychic chaos within by placing contradictory expectations and demands on the inmate. These in turn, far from reducing the "effectivensss" of the prison, function as control measures, intentional or not, by keeping prisoners in a variety of binds—some of which become permanent, all of which produce instability and frustration.

Consider the following: Inmate Russell Collins was being returned to court to testify on his own behalf in a suit he had brought against the New Hampshire State Prison. The room was done largely in dark wood paneling. The chairs were of the prenaugahyde period with real leather profusely attached to solid, deep-grained wood. Strangely reminiscent of those demonstrations where the police outnumbered the demonstrators, one got the feeling that the attendants at these proceedings could start their own legal system if pressed. They brought water to and adjusted the microphone for the witness. Collins was seen, as evidenced by the special attention he received, as someone who could only do his best under advantageous, non-threatening circumstances. He was given bodily as well as psychological comforts. When it was perceived that the "community" of interested spectators could not hear him, a remedy was immediately affected. What he said was taken to be very significant and not to be tampered with.

This witness had recently been released from 30 days and nights in a six-by-eight-foot cell, where he had been stripped almost naked, where he received one meal a day—the other two consisting of a few slices of dry bread—where his only comfort in the way of furnishings was a mattress given him at 3 o'clock in the afternoon and removed again at 7 o'clock in the morning, and where he could receive no visitors, neither write nor receive letters, had no reading material and was treated by a doctor through the bars of his cell.

It might be argued that the contrast between the few hours in that elegant courtroom and the area in which he had recently spent 43 thousand, 200 minutes would itself provide sufficient evidence of the obscene nature of his confinement as well as the readiness of our society to remedy it. However, the question

45

before the judge on that day in Federal Court was not whether Russell Collins was treated in a manner violating every ounce of our good, noble, and even common-sense upbringing. Not at all—the question before the judge was whether or not, in deciding to put him in what staff and inmate alike call the "hole," the prison administrators had followed proper procedures. (It was decided that they had not and so the defense, if not the inmate, rested.)[a]

Other authors [Carter, Glaser, Wilkins, 1972, p. xi] have commented on the fragmentation of our criminal justice process. They have referred to separate administrative entities that are self-serving rather than being constructively related to a larger system. On that day in Fifth Circuit Court, however, a deeper fragmentation than the merely administrative began to appear to us: what we *do* to our social rejects and how we justify it both to them and the public may have built-in contradictions so antithetical to the well-being of the inmate that once he begins his career in that system he must either accept the unacceptable or suffer the consequences.

Sykes [1958], among many, points out that one of the most debilitating pains of imprisonment is the loss of autonomy. The loss of autonomy in itself, however, is not the real source of anguish. The contradiction between the actual condition of the inmate, absolute dependence, and demands placed on him to act as though he weren't, is the source of the most meaningful deprivation. We will begin with the notion of the self as it relates to the historic context in which prisons fulfill their punitive role.

What is it to deprive a man of his freedom? What are we doing when we sentence someone to a three-year or life jail sentence? In confronting the question, we cannot distinguish the normative and the factual historically—that is, what we do and the reasons given for our behavior are inextricably bound. Freedom and its expression are intimately linked to their particular social and historical context. And it is only by considering how a man may express his freedom in that context that we can consider how to divest him of it.

To be exiled from the city–state was considered the worst of treatments by the Athenians simply because freedom meant the ability to take part in the life of the polis. Philoctetes in Sophocles' play describes himself when he is exiled as "friendless, desolate, citiless, cut off from any political community, a corpse among the living." Banishment in other cultures meant nothing more than refusing the "evil-doer" the right to participate in particular ceremonies. For it was participation in these occasions that marked a person's essential character as a full member of the group and thus a free individual [von Hentig, 1937, p. 17].[b] This aspect of our social identity remains in force today. In 1973, for

---

[a]C72-114, District of New Hampshire. Collins vs. Hancock.

[b]"Society's simplest form of self-defence is outlawry . . . the individual's greatest good is his share in a community of peace and law . . . exclusion from the group implies helplessness and destruction as well."

example, the inmates at the Vermont State Prison claimed the right to participate in local elections. In the ensuing uproar, one outraged local politician demanded to know, "What are we doing to punish these men?"

Commenting on the change between the eighteenth- and nineteenth-century
conception of freedom, Simmel suggests that freedom in the former was based
on the notion of the common quality of man *per se*. The nineteenth and
twentieth centuries have been characterized by what he refers to as the "search
for inequality":

> Now the individual that thus became independent also wished to distin-
> guish himself from other individuals. The important point no longer
> was the fact that he was a free individual as such, but that he was
> this specific irreplaceable, given individual. [Simmel, 1950, p. 68]

Thus, to lose freedom is to lose one's definition of oneself as a separate and
identifiable human being. It is no wonder that much of the critical sociological
literature on organizations and institutions is based on the loss of individuality
they entail. But the pangs of such a loss are variable and are an indictment only
under the assumption that being a "specific, irreplaceable, given individual" is a
desirable goal, and any organizational arrangement defeating this goal is pernicious. In fact, with a consistency bordering on the universal, inmates in
Western civilizations feel precisely such pangs. Cohen and Taylor [1972] point
out that a key theme in prison literature is that one had to remain alive and
unchanged. Bettleheim describes his reaction to incarceration in a Nazi camp
in similar terms:

> ... if I should try to sum up in one sentence what my main problem
> was during the whole time I spent in the camp it would be: to pro-
> tect my inner self in such a way that if by any good fortune, I should
> regain liberty, I would be approximately the same person I was when
> deprived of liberty. [Bettleheim, 1960, p. 3]

As one inmate told us about his brief experiences out of prison: "The guys
kid me about not being my old self and then I have to do something to show
everyone that I haven't changed. I have to get in trouble to prove I'm still myself." The question of being "still myself" seems to be as salient outside, if not
more so, as when the inmate was institutionalized. Efforts at being oneself,
according to this inmate, accounted for his continual inability to stay out of
prison once released.

At meetings to determine whether to transfer inmates from the maximum-
to medium-security prisons, the key question was, "Do you feel you are a different person than when you entered this prison?" When inmates murmured
"yes," one felt a correct button being pushed, and if the "yes" was convincing
enough, the transfers were generally accepted. One prisoner told us that in

these jails it was not the physical brutality that bothered him but the way "they messed with your mind." It is this process of "messing" with the minds of inmates—imposing often alien and unsupported self-images or enforcing petty disciplinary rulings in random ways—that provides one of the more disturbing penal conflicts. It has the effect of keeping the inmate busy "dealing" with the institution rather than himself in any constructive manner.

A common personality we saw was that of the insolent inmate forever engaged in psychic battle with guards, other inmates, members of the treatment teams, and all levels of the prison administration. But this is not a simple one-on-one confrontation between him and the "world." It is also between conflicting aspects of his own personality structure. For many of those we interviewed saw at least *some* basic flaws in their socialization and genuinely wanted to change themselves. But this more constructive conflict was necessarily subsumed in the face of the more pressing conflict with the prison itself—an ongoing struggle for some form of self-esteem and pride. Far from the prison wanting to change damaging aspects of the inmate's character, it is designed to attack the *core* of his personality.

If we substitute the term "inmate" for "patient" and "prison" for "analyst," Erickson's description of the dilemma of the mental patient describes that of the inmates:

> We see here the most extreme form of what may be called identity resistance which is, in its milder and more usual forms, the [inmate's] fear that the [prison] . . . may destroy the weak core of the [inmate's] identity and impose his own. [Erickson, 1956, pp. 58–112]

This may be said to parallel a fear common among the poor, especially the non-white. Their fear stems from more than simple identity loss when faced with such programs as the aforementioned ferreting out of "imperfect" children. It continues with moves, which receive far more support than the entire zero population movement, to sterilize welfare mothers. And it parallels the various degrading psychic battles between investigating social workers and their clients. The point of concern here is that a positive self-image for the inmate has more to do with *overcoming* that obtained by virtue of being a member of the prison community (or in Erickson's example, a mental patient) than being anything else. Such considerations should make us shrink from our congratulatory reflex upon hearing routine statements such as the following praise for a new program of "rehabilitation" by a prison administrator:

> One key to the program's success . . . is that the men acquire a new attitude and self-image at the same time that they acquire skills.
> [*The New York Times*, Dec. 13, 1972]

The prison is so structured and oriented that there is an active and purpose-ful program to convince the inmate that he may only have a "good" life when he denounces what and who he is. He must, in the long run, either feign self-ignorance or gain it. The prison in its rules and regulations alone insures that gaining it is no difficult task. The sting of identity transformation, which is the goal of such institutions, is not relieved by referring to its effects as a "new self-image," which is more congenial to the liberal reformist. The inmates, as we will now show, have good reason to fear or, at best, be skeptical of such identity transformations.

Crime As Disease

As Rothman points out in tracing the development of the modern prison, the idea of environmentally produced deviance was the rationale that reformers of the nineteenth century used in arguing for a new penal system. Where the eighteenth-century guardian of law and order found that "the fault rested more with the offender than with the society," the nineteenth-century reformer saw the causes of crime in the environment:

> In their search for the roots of deviant behavior, investigators con-centrated on the convict's upbringing. . . . No matter at what age the deviant committed an offense, the cause could be traced back to his childhood. [Rothman, 1971, p. 64]

Like most reform movements, though, the nineteenth-century ideology of "socializing" the problem did not discard the eighteenth-century's emphasis on the individual but transformed it. By the twentieth century, it is still the indi-vidual "deviant" who feels the wrath of society, but now for reasons over which he has no control.

Secondly, by locating the individual's problem in his environment, the ideology of reform essentially changed the character of the inmate. He became a litmus paper—picking up and displaying not himself but a malevolent environ-ment. This paved the way for hopeful reforms whereby the "deviant" will merely acquire a new self-image through "beneficial" incarceration.

It is, interestingly, only by *accepting* this ideology that mainstream critics of the prison can generate their attacks. A common phrase employed by such critics is that prisons are "colleges of crime." These people do not argue with the assumption that prisons are a place likely to produce new social identities. They argue that the identities thus learned are malevolent—that is, by asso-ciating with other 'hardened' criminals, one "catches" their criminal ways.

One must inspect more closely this "germ theory" of criminality, which, in the sociological literature, usually falls under the rubric of differential association [Cohen, 1955].[c] The germ theory seems to imply a reciprocal arrangement between host and microbe. Translated into social terms, the presupposition is that crime or criminality can be "caught," given that the host is open to new life patterns, i.e., is uncommitted to his "self." Thus, such reformist criticism of penal institutions presupposes that the social self of the inmate is tenuous at best. They argue that who he is makes no difference to how he will respond to his environment.

This last is a critical implication of the germ theory. When persons belonging to different socio-economic groups catch a disease, their bodies manifest the same sort of physiological derangements. If in fact we say that crime can be caught as one catches the measles, we are saying that crime itself can know no distinctions between persons. Thus, those institutions that are charged with curing the "disease" are acting appropriately when they divest the individual of the notion that who he is does make a difference. Here the impersonal, bureaucratic approach of prisons is given an inadvertent boost in its actions from the scientific method itself.

Finally, the application of the germ theory is so widespread that one finds that most of what passes for prison reform today is ultimately a mechanism for finding and isolating the "hard core" germ carriers and placing them in ultra high-security areas. (The initial conception of segregating inmates from society was to protect the *inmates*; to keep them "secure"; however, it has not proven an impossibly difficult step to change the rationales of the penitentiary toward the end of making the public "secure.") The high-security areas are far removed from outside populations and the inmates put on a totally controlled routine. Yet, as we saw in our opening chapter, the notion of what constitutes "hard core," punishable behavior is a political and economic matter; not some purified form of objective pathology (see also Chapter 7). The germ theory of criminality attempts to artificially transcend the political nature of deviancy and is used to justify the near total isolation of certain people from society. One contemporary spokesman [Banfield, 1968, ch. 8] suggests that it is possible to determine the *likelihood* of a youngster committing crimes in the future. His program is to have the state *immediately* begin to curtail his freedom. Realizing

---

[c]Cohen argues that in fact delinquent subcultures arise and legitimize behaviors in reaction to the inability to measure up to middle-class standards. "Young people of different social classes, race, and ethnicity find themselves competing with one another for status.... However, they are not all equally well-equipped for success..." While this may be factually correct, the point, of course, is that such analysis tends to solidify the notion that "success" is predicated on some personal quality that "delinquents" have failed to obtain due to "poor-socialization." We have no doubt that Cohen can narrowly demonstrate the accuracy of this account. What we are pointing out, however, is the way such accounts are put to use by correctional "reformers."

that this scheme might raise a few eyebrows among the soft-headed, he retorts in a persuasive if circular manner:

> In any event, if abridging the freedom of persons who have not committed crimes is incompatible with the principles of free society, so, also, is the presence in such society of persons who, if their freedom is not abridged, would use it to inflict serious injuries on others. [Banfield, 1968, p. 184]

Such are the implications of the germ theory—the diseased deviant—of crime carried out to its logical conclusions.

Fromm's deprecatory description of "mass man" fits what criminologist and penologist argue is essential to understanding the character of the inmate *at least with regard to his criminal ways.*

> [He] does not experience himself as the active bearer of his own powers and richness, but as an impoverished "thing" dependent on powers outside of himself, unto whom he has projected his living substance. [Fromm, 1955, p. 124]

Such a personality is obviously to be avoided in the society at large. Yet behind bars, the inmate must embrace this as a description of his essential self prior to being seen as a *bona fide* member of the prison community. We must be clear here. Fromm's statement is a factual account of the world as he sees it. Penal advocates of the germ theory of crime, however, use the description normatively—that is, this *should* be the inmate's view of himself, and the structure of the prison is to be understood as validating that description.

In an environment having as its operating model the constant question of who one *is,* "security" checks are a constant presence. We sat in on disciplinary meetings in which an inmate would be called in as a witness, give his written pass with his name and permission times on it to the guard in the room, give perhaps a half-minute testimony (which was, as we discuss in Chapter 5, invariably dismissed as inconclusive), reach up, get that piece of paper, and leave the room.

Although there are no women inmates at the state facility, all women who visit their husbands or boyfriends have to be stamped before entering the visiting room and checked again upon leaving. The fact that such checks are done seemingly at random only heightens the tension felt therein. For example, *much* of what goes on in the treatment of inmates has a random quality, and psychologists have pointed out that events that are perceived as unpleasant are known to produce much more anxiety when they occur at random than do similar events that occur in a systematic fashion. Thus, while penologists have used sociological and psychological literature, their use has been

highly selective. (For a review of this literature see Appley and Trumbull
[1967].)

The physical security checks are the more mundane mirrors of the emo-
tional and psychological security checks prisons constantly impose on their
members. The inmates are in fact in a state of total dependence on the prison
staff, from the essentials of life to those little slips of paper allowing them to
move around. Yet by punishing them in the first place, the state must have
made the supposition that they had acted criminally in a more or less free manner—that is, they were not completely dependent creatures. When the notion
of "rehabilitation" is mixed in with punishment, the need for the inmate to
perform as a free and "active bearer" of his life decision stands out in even
starker contrast to his reality of almost total institutional dependence.

The inmate, then, who succeeds at passing the security checks of the
prison does so either by being a good performer or by being inauthentic.[d] If
he claims to be an autonomous human being, he must also lay claim to the
immoral self the authorities claim for him while simultaneously claiming that
he could never have been the author of his own behavior, because that is precisely what the germ theory entails. Like Faulkner's Joe Christmas, he *must*
believe "with calm paradox that he was the volitionless servant of the fatality
in which he believed he did not believe" [Faulkner, 1932, p. 97].

Many authors talking about institutions in general or prisons in particular
have stressed their characteristic process of depersonalization. This is what
Goffman [1961] has called the process of "role dispossession." Those characteristics of the inmate that distinguish him in the outside world are symbolically stripped away and leave him just like any other inmate. The deteriora-
tion we found among inmates having served time in prison, however, cannot be
accounted for in terms of this process alone. For the fact is that many other
institutions engage in a similar process and do not produce a population that
can be characterized as psychologically impaired. Rather, the impairment is to
be accounted for in terms of the *interplay* between this process of depersonalization on one hand and the demand for autonomy exerted by prison personnel
on the other.

One of the most glaring examples of an inmate whose entire career through
the institution was an effort to maintain his social identify was Mr. M. This
inmate was highly educated and, in fact, had been a probation officer in a
neighboring state prior to his conviction for a sexual offense. When we first
met him, he refused to cooperate with our study concerning the psychological
and social adjustments of inmates. He was quick to point out that far from

---

[d]"Inauthenticity is not only a more or less deliberate determination to act in conflict
with one's own core nature; much more pervasive and pernicious are the modes of life by
which we act out of harmony with that nature because of self-ignorance. Sometimes we
remain unaware of what we are at the core because we are manipulated by others. Sometimes we are self-deceived" [Kaufman, 1971, pp. 191–106].

being useful to the project, he was so different from "the ordinary inmate here" that it would be counterproductive to use him. In some sense, he was right, for his education, I.Q., and occupational status were all far beyond the mean. In more meaningful senses, however, he was wrong.

From the outset, Mr. M believed that he was different and that the differences were ones that counted. Further, survival for Mr. M, like the inmates seen by Taylor and Cohen [1972] as well as for Dr. Bettleheim [1960] himself, was to be measured by his success at maintaining the saliency of the status arrangements that characterized him prior to his incarceration. Furthermore, far from denying the saliency of these differences, the prison officials themselves lent some measure of credence to them by asking him to take over the management of the prison's internal bookkeeping. This was a position not ordinarily assigned to an inmate and was one requiring much responsibility. Concretely, then, it would appear that this inmate had managed to escape the depersonalization process and could thus be expected to escape what critics claim are the prison's most debilitating effects.

But far from escaping these effects, Mr. M, on leaving the prison, had so deteriorated that he was characterized by one psychiatrist as suffering from paranoia. The change in personality was so marked that it deserves comment. On first meeting this man we were struck by his sense of control and calm. He appeared well in command of himself and his situation. We next saw him two days before his release date. He was suffering from high blood pressure, severe headaches, and nose bleeds of a psychosomatic nature. He spent over an hour denouncing the prison authorities; he claimed he was going to take his case to the United Nations. What had happened?

Having escaped the "stripping" process, Mr. M nevertheless had not escaped the psychological impact this process is said to produce. In order to understand this, it is necessary to step back and consider just what a social identity entails. The critical point is that the concrete character of a personal identity is not as important as the locus for establishing it. In short, by *necessarily* transferring the power to establish the salience of his accomplishments within the prison to the prison authorities, Mr. M lost the very potency of that identity for whatever good it would do in terms of self-esteem. While remaining "himself," he spoiled any measure of benefit that self could bring him. While clinging to an authentic self, he had to give over to others the final stamp of approval. In a sense, his self became a currency whose value fluctuated as a function of a uniquely fickle market place. In sum, in spite of outward appearances, it lost all intrinsic value.

It should be noted that we are not making a blanket condemnation of the value of a new self-image for many inmates. Quite a few of those to whom we spoke displayed a genuine sense of inadequacy that runs counter to the "tough guy" image that has been popularized. In fact, if one had to pick out any single adjective to characterize them, it would be "inadequate." What we are stressing here, however, is the fact that prisons *cannot* instill a sense of self in any

constructive way. We are arguing that it is precisely *not* the goal of the institution to give a sense of self, but rather to deny it. Granting this, it becomes the
central and most pressing task for an inmate to show himself as one who has no
commitment to his own existence. This is to put on, at least initially, a performance.

Sadly, it is a no-win task for the inmate. For, if he succeeds, he will likely
be cemented into that performance—into a self that is relevant only to his self
as a prison member. If he fails, he will be repudiated by the institution and
made to suffer additional confinements. The prison, not unmindful that this
new self may be mere impersonation, has set up "security checks" that have the
effect of leaving the inmate little time to do anything else but maintain this
inauthentic front. Nowadays, such checks include "progress" reports to the
warden, "counseling," and the like. Insofar as the state holds crime to be an
effect of one's environment—independent of any essential character of inmates—
we will have a prison structure whose main task is to display the adequacy of
that account of prisoners. In order to make his way through prison, the inmate
must at least pretend to disassociate his behavior from himself. It is no new
comment to point out that an act long sustained and reinforced may become,
at some point, no longer an act. So the same class of people who are bounced
back and forth between the street and jail are, in effect, conditioned to accept
this bouncing. Many end up acting in ways appropriate to this ideology, and
the "mysterious" cycle of long prison records continues unabated.

Catching Hell

If one cannot turn to prison authorities for adequate confirmation of self,
there are two alternative sources open to new inmates. These are the outside
community from which he just came and to which 97 percent return, or the
prison community itself. However, the former is severely curtailed by the
security regulations of the prison, and the latter has built-in hazards and limitations. For example, at the time of this writing, *all* mail either to or from inmates
at the New Hampshire State Prison is read by one of the custodians. Much of
what passes for materials required to be recorded on the inmate's record is purely
sexual in nature and could hardly be seen as a security threat. Secondly, there
is the habit of turning away visitors and mail without informing the inmate.
Edgar Schein [1960, pp. 148-161] discusses the uses of very similar techniques
by the Chinese during the Korean engagement.

The basis of the difficulties in establishing decent personal contacts behind
bars grows out of a nearly universal acceptance of the germ theory of criminality.
This theory has two basic assumptions: (1) that one's sense of self is totally
dependent upon one's relations with others; and (2) that the self in question is
so weak and plastic that regardless of the kind of self originally entering these

contacts the effects will be the same. We have already discussed how the application and use of the germ theory has the tendency to level and depersonalize the inmate population. There are further difficulties. One author says:

> Any person can learn any pattern of behavior which he is able to execute. He inevitably assimilates behavior from the surrounding culture. . . . Since criminal behavior is thus developed in association with criminals it means that *crime is the cause of crime* [6]. (Our emphasis) The idea that criminality is a consequence of an excess of intimate associations with criminal behavior patterns is valuable because . . . it negates assertions that deviation from norms is simply a product of being emotionally insecure . . . and then indicates in a general way why only some emotionally insecure persons . . . commit crimes. [Creesy, 1964, p. 76]

Although virtually none of the inmates we saw had read a sociological text, their ideas about association mirror much of what is promulgated in those learned books—that is, they accept some variant of the germ theory. From the outset, then, new inmates have cultural baggage that acts as a restraint on personal relations. There is nothing in the prison structure that acts as a deterrent to these assumptions, and much of what the authorities do with regard to the personal relations of inmates is legitimized by these assumptions. It is a matter of equal importance to sociologists, prison administrators, and new inmates to prevent relations from reaching the point of intimacy, i.e., being "sufficiently close" as to present a threat.

In discussing with new inmates what they saw as one of their largest problems in the institution, we were impressed with the frequency with which they made pronouncements like the following:

> You get to know these guys but you don't want to know them too well. It can't do you any good in the long run here to make friends.

Here the inmate is caught on the horns of a dilemma in which he gets gored no matter what he does. Believing that most inmates are both bad and contagious, the administration isolates them. Sharing this belief, many of the inmates (though the percentage is noticeably smaller) isolate *themselves* but form moving coalitions for protection or obtaining of scarce resources. But the relations remain mockeries of what we normally call friendship. If the inmate plays it safe, he will, at the very least, be lonely—often pathologically so.

Others have touched on this aspect of imprisonment. Their stress is on the prison structure and how it enforces "psychological solitary confinement." Cloward [1956], for example, points out that incentives such as parole "good time" allowances and privileges of various sorts are administered as rewards to inmates who heed the administrator's admonition to "do your own time." In

discussing the almost miraculous rehabilitation of an inmate, one of the officers
we saw was quick to underscore the point that, "E——-stays away from everyone
and minds his own business." Parallels to this normative aspect of "unique individuality" can be found in psychiatric literature. But far from being seen as
expected and rewarded behavior, as it is in prison, it is rightly taken as a pathology.

> ... the delusion of unique individuality cuts off all communication
> that is not absolutely required by maturing necessities. . . . Other
> people are treated as troublesome units transiently more or less useful
> to a flaming ambition to outdo everyone else in some particular field
> of accomplishment. [Sullivan, 1937, pp. 848–861]

So, for example, "other people are treated as troublesome units transiently
more or less useful," from the prison's point of view is translated as "you owe
nothing to these other guys, do your own time." From the inmate's point of
view it translates as, "These guys can only get you into trouble. . . . I must
leave them alone." The "delusion of unique individuality" is also something of
a reflection of our society's myth of the perfect capitalist. He is one who seeks
his own financial benefit without significant harm to or dependence upon
others [Spenser, 3rd ed., 1712].[e] This character's needs and aspirations form
the basis of much of American economic theory and social justification [de
Tocqueville, 1840].[f] Of course, he does not and never has existed. No one can
be so isolated in a competitive society; for when one person gains, almost inevitably someone else loses. But, to some, it is a comforting and sustaining myth.

It is worthwhile to note that an inmate will tell you where the dope is
planted, how often he uses those drugs, and how to make illegal home-brew
before he will tell you who his friends are. We may either conclude he has no
friends or that in revealing who they are he will place himself (or them) in more
jeopardy than he will by blatantly revealing illegal aspects of his prison life.
Either way, the need for affiliation is blunted in rather staggering fashion. The
world is turned upside down. If friendship is a symptom of mental health in

----

[e]P.S. Spenser could be directing the affairs of the modern correctional officer when
he addresses men of the business world: "He (the knowing man) is blind in no man's cause,
but best sighted in his own." "He confines himself to the circle of his own affairs and
thrusts not his fingers into needless fires. He sees the falseness of it [the world] and therefore learns to trust himself ever" [Spenser, 1712, p. 111].

[f]de Tocqueville graphically describes the result: "[Americans of the nineteenth
century] . . . owe nothing to any man; they expect nothing from any man; they acquire
the habit of always considering themselves as standing alone, and they are apt to imagine
that their whole destiny is in their own hands."

"Thus not only does democracy make every man forget his ancestors, but it hides his
descendants and separates his contemporaries from him; it throws him back forever upon
himself alone and threatens in the end to confine him entirely within the solitude of his
own heart."

the outside world, it is viewed as a symptom of pending deviance inside the walls. In New Hampshire, inmates have a satire on what the custodians see in inmate relations: "One guy alone in the yard is a nut; two guys together and they're fairies; three guys together is a riot."

In the Attica report, for example, the most suspected group—much prior to the riot—were the Black Muslims; not for any overt behaviors on their part, but simply because they manifested a degree of intimacy and comradery beyond what prison officials felt to be a "safe" level. Of course, as it turned out, they were the most careful with the lives of the hostages and had developed enough social organization to act with some effectiveness during the turmoil [*Attica: The Official Report of the New York State Special Commission on Attica*, 1972]. Commission of Corrections Russell Oswald confirms that during the revolt, the Muslims saved the lives of the hostages and were responsible for his safe return after he agreed to negotiate with inmates. What he does not tell us is that for the previous 12 years, the New York Department of Corrections kept a list of all inmates belonging to the Muslim faith, which was forwarded to the State Police for use in a *subversive* file [*Attica*, 1972, p. 123; for Oswald's comments on the Muslims see *Attica, My Story*, 1972].

Further, the near absolute power exerted over inmates ensures that what is considered proper behavior for inmates translates immediately into what they must in fact do. Two inmates may live side by side for years. They share the same occupation, conditions, and facilities. Once released on parole, however, being seen in each other's company is cause for revocation of parole. Furthermore, most jurisdictions have strict rules against an ex-inmate visiting someone still confined, whether the visitor is still on parole or not. Although this rule was officially changed in Vermont in 1972, inmates charge that such visits are still "discouraged" [Luparar, June, 1972]. Proximity in the prison is taken to be "safe" only if it is just that—proximity. And, given the power of those in power, it remains just that. Once out of the official's legal grasp, proximity can potentially become intimacy. And as the "germ theory" holds, intimacy between deviants produces move deviancy.

Speaking about attenuated social encounters, Goffman says:

> . . . persons present are likely to feel uneasy. . . . A person who chronically makes himself or others uneasy in conversation and perpetually kills encounters is a faulty interactant, he is likely to have such a baleful effect upon the social life around him that he may just as well be called a faulty person. [Goffman, 1957, Vol. 10, pp. 47–60]

As in other areas, prison structure turns a prescription for normal behavior on its head. Rather than requiring an encounter to be fulfilled, prison routine encourages encounters that *must* fail. The effect is to produce what Goffman calls "faulty persons," and who wants such a person for a friend! Thus, the prison produces the very community the inmate has been told to expect upon arrival. By gearing his behavior to this description, the inmate participates in and fulfills the friendless self-fulfilling prophecy that is the modern prison.

This may well be the single most difficult aspect of inmate life. ". . . the very mark of the most extreme exploitation and degradation is that the victims see themselves as the exploiters see them" [Connolly, 1971, Vol. 14, p. 246]. In so doing, they help not only to sustain those very conditions that contribute to their own incarceration but also to legitimize their being given such treatment in the first place—that is, they become "institutionalized." In its most extreme forms, institutionalization leads to inmates who actually seem to have made a fairly permanent peace with their surroundings. There is no stronger indictment of our penal system. In its more usual forms, this sort of institutionalization leads to the inmate accepting the prison's notion of himself as an unworthy character and thus continuing in an obvious way his life cycle of perpetual incarceration. A parallel form of self-hatred has been unearthed by the movement for liberation of women and blacks, and it occurs among ethnic groups with great regularity. It can paralyze. But, as those movements have shown, it is not permanent and, when transcended, can have exhilarating, explosive effects both in and out of our visible prisons.

When the process of desocialization is found in the community at large, it is often associated with increased emphasis on individuation—that is, "the ideal of the moral autarchy of the individual. . ."

> the ideal of perfection in a strong, self-sufficient person who is not incomplete in solitude and who is not craving for anything let alone friendship. [Halmos, 1953, p. 108]

Usually, however, this ideal obtains against a backdrop of social supports. In our prisons, which are among our last bastions of the idea of the insurmountable, free individual, these supports are not only absent, there is also a systematic attempt to deny the possibility of their existence. It is Calvinism without the promise of a heaven.

When speaking of privacy and reserve as enforced in the institution and thus converting them into solitude and withdrawal, we are not advocating the "extremism of the individualist" so characteristic of competitive liberalism. What we are attempting to show is how this ideology penetrates penal institutions. Even if one were to accept the individualistic philosophy that distinguishes penal approaches, one would have to recognize that in practice the administration systematically undercuts the very supports this rationale requires.

One of the basic features of prison life is the absence of the necessary conditions that promote a real privacy and real reserve. Instead, it presents an artificial counterpart to these conditions that results in social isolation rather than privacy and psychological withdrawal rather than reserve.

Again, a parallel with the ideology of our economic system can be drawn. Our economy *theoretically* works with isolated financial entities; each works to maximize its own well-being by serving some public need. Thus, the society subsidizes them only in as much as it purchases their products, and so those corporate entities are said to represent nothing more than the public will, freely and democratically expressed in the market place. There are, of course, massive difficulties with this view, but we can leave them aside for our purposes and simply point out that there is no major corporation that could exist today without government contracts or backing in some other form. The instances of the Pentagon bailing out ailing companies or the government bailing out such firms as Boeing or Lockheed are only the more sensational cases of this general phenomena. What is of interest to us here is simply that the *ideology* of the free, autonomous private corporation persists. Corporate executives, while obviously recognizing that they are, in effect, on the public dole, do not *feel* the stigma of being on welfare. Our tradition of accepting the basic tenets of capitalism—Calvinism in the consumer goods division—supplies them with the needed social supports that those *individuals* on welfare lack. An artist who isolates herself for weeks at a time knows that it is socially acceptable to do so, and she thereby transforms isolation into privacy. An inmate has no such knowledge and no way of obtaining it.

In Search of a Friend

Writing about survival problems in another situation, one author stresses the importance of a companion:

> I began to think back on the physical presence, the point of reference, the sort of ever present life belt which my companion had repre- sented. . . . . Amidst the loneliness everything seemed unreal and mocking. I felt a terrible need for human company. [Bombard, 1954, p. 81]

To survive means having some way of "knowing what is happening to you," and so knowing means having some means at one's disposal for objectifying the experience. But isolation of prisoners from one another in acceptance of the carnard that deviancy is contagious leaves them without one of the most documented and probably critical functions of affiliation—feedback. To have a friend is to have some mechanism for testing one's relation to reality. As soon as one is convinced of the germ theory, the resultant communication void de- prives one of a benchmark for measuring one's own progress or assessing the most basic parameters of one's current situation. Even when the disaster is not directly personal, turning to friends is one of the most modal patterns of adaptation. The National Opinion Research Corporation, for example, found that on hearing of the death of President Kennedy, 54 percent of the public said they "felt like talking about it with other people" [Sheatsley and Feldman, 1964, Vol. 28, No. 2, pp. 189-215].

As in so many other areas, however, the new inmate's situation has a double bind. The "disaster" that has occurred to him is in part defined by having been divested of "normal" social interaction as he sees it. *The very character of the situation precludes the hope of finding someone "to talk to."* And there is further trouble in store. For some of the inmates transcend this form of conditioning. They have come to grips with at least some of the traps laid in their path and are actively trying to confront them. One of the characteristics they share is their relatively healthy interactions with other inmates. They are commonly referred to as "jailhouse lawyers" and, eventually, by administrations, as "troublemakers" (not entirely unlike those who have raised their consciousness on the outside).

We interviewed a number of these men and were impressed by their general spirit of resistance, their articulateness, and most of all by their relative lack of skepticism and/or fear of their fellow inmates. They were skeptical in highly *selective* ways, as one would expect from a rational creature. These men have kept their mental health by refusing to internalize anxieties and instead have vocalized and outwardly directed their energies. In so doing, however, they are likely to incur the wrath of those charged with their incarceration. Thus, they often receive punishments—various forms of solitary confinement—within the prison. By refusing to accept the unacceptable, they are made to suffer the consequences. More vulnerable inmates are told in no uncertain terms to avoid such inmates, and so the cycle of perpetually induced isolation is perpetuated. In a sense, all inmates suffer from structurally induced schizophrenia. For if we consult what schizophrenia entails, we will see that it bears a remarkable resemblance to the organizational program for inmates:

> The term schizoid refers to an individual the totality of whose experience is split in two main ways; in the first place, there is a rent in his relation with the world, and in the second there is a disruption of his relation with himself. Such a person is not able to experience himself "together with" others or "at home" in the world, but on the contrary, he experiences himself in his pairing aloneness and isolation. [Laing, 1965, p. 1]

From the administration's point of view, "the man who stays content in his own chamber has risen above the feeble and mortal condition of the many" [Halmos, 1953, p. 116]. But even this nearly impossible state of affairs is curtailed by the security considerations pervading every aspect of prison life, for this model entails the possibility of privacy that is totally missing from the prisoner's existence. In the New Hampshire State Prison, for example, there is not a single toilet available to the inmate that does not have at the least, a window in the door. The overwhelming majority are merely in the cell, which is open to an adjacent walkway. In some circumstances, one may be willing to give up privacy for some larger good to thus divest the process of any feeling of mortification. In jail, however, no such neutralizing efforts are made. Quite the opposite. It is held that the prisoners' lack of privacy is maintained because of the administration's need to maintain *security*.[g]

"Evidently the man of a serene and solid *Weltanschauung* is held to be self-sufficient in his aloneness, finding comfort with ease in the contemplation of revealed truth, beauty and goodness" [Halmos, 1953, p. 116]. The inmates, though, are not felt to be so endowed. Instead, what the inmate does when he is actually alone is a potential threat to the institution. He is given the task of the "indomitable individual" but deprived of the individualist's character or achievements.

The phenomena of using the private for public purposes is not confined to those who are legally incarcerated. Recent revelations of political spying and taping are but the most newsworthy aspects of this. It has been a practice for many years, for example, for corporations to monitor the bathrooms of their own employees, while advertisements disturb the privacy of public bathrooms. The thousands of commercial messages we have thrown at us daily, in all the media and on public roads, are other instances of this lack of respect for our privacy. It seems not entirely unreasonable to suggest that much of the defacing graffiti we see on billboards is a form of protest against those invasions of privacy. Such protests are being mirrored behind bars as well. During the time of our study, the most common charge in the prison's disciplinary hearing concerned the refusal of inmates to submit to a strip search. Such activities both directly and symbolically open the inmate to privacy-depriving scrutiny and are being more openly challenged by inmates.

The Mythology of Autonomy and Its Risks

As previously stated, the most common complaint of those writing about the prison scene is the lack of autonomy suffered by inmates. It is clear that

---

[g]Even communication channels normally considered private are felt by inmates to be invaded with impunity by the prison administration. For example, a cartoon in the prison newsletter shows an inmate talking to a staff psychiatrist who is holding a tape recording machine. The caption is: "Before I interview you all, here's the Miranda warning, boy."

Every high ranking prison official to whom we spoke held that (1) it was perfectly legitimate for counselors and psychiatrists to tell the administration everything an inmate had confided to them, and (2) even though most inmates were fully aware of this practice that it would not interfere with their "therapy."

the *structure* of the prison does in fact make the inmate totally dependent on itself. But the prison must also hold out the *ideology* of and hence demand for some form of autonomy. Hence the prison must make every effort to convince the prisoner of two things: (1) that his efforts alone can win him early release, and (2) that other inmates can only impede his progress through the system.

Some results of this conditioning can be at least tentatively suggested by noting that over half of the inmates at the facilities where this work was done reported (a) that they could not trust others, (b) that they never visit or seek out other inmates, and (c) that they had no one to whom they could tell their personal and/or legal troubles.

Conclusion

Paradoxically, by stressing autonomy from other inmates, the prison runs the risk of normatively mitigating its own control. Ironically, steps taken to "protect" the prisoner from criminal contamination may result in a threat to the institution itself. For, if the inmate is supposed to become the kind of person who is unaffected by others around him, then those others can conceivably include the prison staff.

Those working in the prison often complained about the inmates who "have no respect for authority of any kind. They won't even listen to their friends." Yet it is precisely this sort of total individualist who is, in some respects, the most rewarded throughout his penal career.

Yet another paradox emerges as a result of the tension between prison structure and ideology. Earlier studies of men in stressful environments have documented the relation between threat and social cohesion:

> The impersonal threat of injury from the enemy affecting all alike, produces a high degree of cohesion so that personal attachments . . . become intensified. . . . Friendships . . . satisfy urges, based on mutual interest and gain. . . . The character of these bonds is of the greatest significance in determining ability to withstand the stresses of the combat situation. [Grinker and Spiegel, 1945, p. 21-22]

This sort of cohesion and its remarkable effects have been seen under aerial bombardment in countries as diverse as England and North Vietnam.

In order to reduce the potential threat of cohesion among inmates, the prison has a choice of either lowering the implicit threat in the prison situation or convincing the inmate that the real threat to him comes from other inmates. Yet one of the most critical implications of the applied ideology of the germ theory is to convince the prisoner that he is "just another con, like everyone else here." But to convince him that the other inmates are "just like him" is also to bring to light their potential as possible allies, united against the prison. This has, in a modified way, occurred. We heard surprising instances of solidarity with those who had made even unsuccessful escape attempts. Although the daily reaction of most inmates to one another is that of distrust, any sort of crisis brought them together in a rather startling display of genuine solidarity. In the racially divided Attica prison, for example, color lines, as barriers, melted. Outside the prisons, the blending together of many diverse political strands under the label of "communist" or "radical" has in fact had the effect of increasing the solidarity of many who, if left alone, would have more disagreements than agreements. It should also be added that part of the basis for the inmates' togetherness—their "all being alike"—is that with regard to their economic background, they *are* all alike. And no small part of their anger and union germinates shortly after the seeding of that realization.

If their criminality—or revolutionary fervor—is contagious, the prison must, as discussed, isolate them from one another. This is to offer a model of a "proper" inmate as not being in need of support; one who can obtain basic needs on his own by being a free and independent individual. And this notion of desired autonomy blends in with the punitive aspect of prison. To convince an inmate of his potential as a free man is the methodology for accomplishing this aspect. For only the potentially autonomous can feel the lack of autonomy.

The ideology of autonomy in conjunction with a social structure whereby inmates must turn to prison authorities for even bare necessities produces an unstable, contradictory system. Yet, as in so many other areas, the people with the least power in that situation, the inmates, are blamed for its existence. It is the unstable, unpredictable, untrustworthy character of the convict that necessitates the intense control characterizing the modern prison.

By using a doctrine that is singularly unsuited to their practices, prison administrators create the very menace they are empowered to "cure." Security is an ever-present issue in the institution, primarily as a result of the logic and social function of the institution itself.

4 The Invisible Prison

> The trend toward the professional view that criminals are sick rather than bad has had as one of its consequences the kind of policy characterizing the treatment oriented prison and the attendant concern for inmates rather than . . . society.
>
> —*Donald R. Creesy, 1961*

As material conditions and the doctrine of the liberal state continue to part ways, incarceration has been alternatively justified in terms of the "treatment" model. As prisons increasingly claim for themselves this treatment orientation, we would expect the prison structure to display organizational characteristics allowing for such treatment. Prisons, then, would look more like service organizations than like manufacturing concerns [Street, Vinter and Perrow, 1966].

Social scientists have usually looked exclusively at the resources needed by organizations not only to stay in business but to thrive. Our stress, however, is on the fact that each and every organization must have at its command resources to handle inevitable mistakes and crises.[a] In short, the vocabulary of success works only insofar as there is a concomitant vocabulary of "realism" whereby a set of beliefs is available to explain why certain moves failed and how such failures can be avoided in the future. (Rue Bucher's [Mimeo, No.] unpublished paper is the only one we know of which systematically accounts for the acquisition of such vocabularies in a professional setting. Another interesting but less intensive account can be found in Donald W. Light [1972, pp. 821–838].) An examination of how institutions *define* and react to such crises is more revealing than an accounting of their routine successes.

The questions we raise are the following: Can prisons claim a kind of professional standing with regard to inmate treatment? Are inmates actually the recipients of services offered by professionals? If so, do these professionals have at their command an organized set of expertise applied in inmate treatment such that the former is accountable to the latter in case of error? In sum, in what sense can it be claimed that the inmate is a full member of the prison as an on-going organization?

Of course, each of these questions can be conveniently answered in the affirmative by simply *assuming* that the ideology and practice of treatment

---

[a]Sykes puts this nicely: "The emergency, then, is a phase to be passed through again and again; and organization is many of these emergencies, these crises, tied together in a recognizable continuity." Unfortunately, he then points out that "riots" are the typical crises in the prison without examining how this comes to be the case. [Sykes, 1958, p. 109]

65

coincide behind bars—however shaky that union may regrettably be. We, however, take this common assumption to be an open, empirical question needing analytic rather than ideologically loaded answers. If one *accepts* this assumption, one must expect the prisons to share definitions of and reactions to institutional crises with other service organizations.

Members and Mistakes

The difference between being a member *of* or merely being physically *in* an organization hinges on whether or not services are actually rendered to the relevant individual, whether any failures in that regard allow the individual to claim as a member of that organization that a mistake has been made, and whether the organization has strategies for dealing with such mistakes [Etzioni, 1964, ch. IX]. In the absence of such factors, we can safely say that the individual in question is not a participant, and therefore the organization's notion of technical competency is never defined in terms of him.

In order, then, to locate the kind of participation that characterizes the inmate's role in the organizational structure of the prison, we need to search out those strategies that the prison maintains to deal with the kinds of mistakes most likely to occur with regard to the inmate himself. *We will find none.*

In the traditional professions two kinds of questions, regarding the profession's treatment of its clients, are "reviewable." The first deals with the ethicality of the professional, which may raise legal questions. As we shall see, the work of prison officials is also susceptible to questions of legality, but there is an important exception: What is reviewable is only the set of practices that violate constitutional law in a context not specific to the prison itself.

The second reviewable area is the competency of the practitioner, which is almost always left to the judgment of fellow professionals. The social control inherent in work review by professionals is exercised within prisons as well, but again there is an important exception: Such reviews are invariably undertaken out of 'earshot' of the inmates. Thus, to the extent that these control mechanisms remain *informal,* the inmate is (1) unlikely to be aware of their existence and (2) ill-equipped to inaugurate such control on his own behalf. An example will underscore this. Prior to the Attica uprising, Commissioner Oswald decided not to concur in what he felt to be an unwise decision by staff personnel. (The decision had been to transfer or otherwise punish rebellious leaders.)

> Although Oswald's decision . . . was regarded as a complete failure by the correction officers, it was not a victory in any sense for the inmates. *They did not know of [the warden's] request for transfer of the inmates or of [Oswald's] reversal of this policy. [Attica: The Official Report, p. 135; italics added.]*

If the warden is to avoid the chaos of a head-on confrontation with the more custodial minded of his employees, informal devices for regulation become mandatory. Thus the sheer notion of *formal* accountability to inmates as clients or members of the maximum security prison and the structural arrangements implied become impossible. This, of course, raises the question of what actual status the inmate has in that organization. If we locate membership in terms of the accountability the organization makes available through regularized procedures and the kinds of mistakes for which the organization can be held accountable, the inmate is neither employer, customer, nor client; he is a non-participant

This is not to say that the prison does not have a *legal* relation to the inmate. But the courts have held that this relation extends only to basic constitutional rights accorded all *"persons"* and is therefore not relevant to the unique circumstances of the inmate. In what was considered a milestone liberal decision, this point was reinforced:

> Federal courts sit not to supervise prisons but to enforce the constitutional rights of all persons, which include prisoners. [Crue vs. Beto, 405 U.S. 319, 321, 1972]

The concrete result of such decisions and subsequent practices is to take what may be the final step in removing from the inmate the status of a member of the organization. As we argued earlier, membership in an organization can be thought of as a process whereby accountability and thus *mistakes are regularized into certain channels.* It is only in terms of membership that notions of "error" or "mistakes" can come into play. For it is only the presence of structural arrangements that allows one to claim organizational membership. And it is only through such membership that one can claim that a mistake has been made towards one by that organization.

Accountability and Error

Implicit in the control of error, therefore, is the notion of accountability. Mistakes hinge not only on notions of competency or success but also on accountability and error, which in turn necessarily make reference to relevant audiences. Bucher (Mimeo N.D.) states that accountability requires an understanding of how the professionals themselves define the issues and how they come to define them. Equally crucial to the understanding of "accountability," however, are the necessary social structures that either impede or enhance some sector of the public's claims that a profession is accountable to them. While this dimension of organization has received some attention with regard to medicine, no prison literature to our knowledge has raised the notion of accountability of prison personnel to inmates. Yet if the claim is that treatment is accorded inmates, one would imagine that accountability becomes relevant.

The crucial point is that since organizations have only a particular audience, they do not make particular kinds of mistakes. This is not to argue that the practices that we call mistakes would not happen, but simply that minus the relevant audience they would not be mistakes and could even be successes. Many government agencies are ostensively established because private, profit organizations would not make mistakes if their only audience or reference group was their stockholders. Certainly the ombudsman movement in the last decade can be regarded as supplying an organizational structure that makes "the public" a relevant audience. Positions such as Affirmative Action Officers in universities can be seen as making salient a *feature* of part of the existing membership of these organizations—in this case sex and minority group status.

Members of service and manufacturing occupations typically use some image of the "ideal" client to fashion a conception of how their work ought to be performed. In the prison, however, there are competing conceptions of the inmate—his character and problems—and thus what ought to be done for or to him.

The modern prison prides itself on the rehabilitation efforts of its staff. This model posits the inmate as a *victim* of circumstances who, when exposed to healthier environments and various "tinkerings,"[b] will become an essentially law-abiding citizen. The inmate is not to be guarded and demeaned but to be helped and understood. The staff, then, of the modern prison has putatively been reconceptualized to meet this new specification of its audience.

One author claims that an important function of the professions is to manage conflict and crises within the social system. ". . . They are called upon to provide non-routine response to potentially non-routine situations" [Elliott, 1972, p. 132]. If this is the case, then one clue to who occupies professional ranks in a prison and the kind of client this entails is both the prevailing definition of what constitutes a crisis and which, given that definition, is considered the relevant group to be called in to handle it.

Sykes [1958, p. 45] reports that, "When the guards at the New Jersey State Prison were asked what topics should be of first importance in a proposed training program, 98 percent picked 'what to do in event of trouble'."

In 1971 and 1972, the officials of the State of New Hampshire decided that prison "troubles" required a new definition. These "troubles" were not the result of bad men acting together but of sick minds. While the diagnosis did not constitute a major shift in ideology, the cure appeared to imply a major shift in prison routine and structure.

---

[b]It is this "tinkering" phenomenon that is new in prisons. In the original design of the penitentiary, it was felt that crucial to the "rehabilitation" of the deviant was that he be left alone. For an exposition of the model, which has been taken over by prisons, see Goffman [1961, p. 333 ff.].

The warden, acting in concert with the state's director of mental health and the state's crime commission, procured a generous one-year federal grant designed to provide "therapeutic services" to disturbed offenders. These services included a team of psychiatrists, social workers, psychiatric nurses, and vocational rehabilitation staff.

What the additional personnel portended was a complete reorganization of the prison structure, since what now constituted "troubles" would fall within the domain of the "helping" professions rather than the custodians—or so these professionals must have assumed.

However, events proved that such a reorganization had not occurred at all. Some 9 months after the onset of the therapeutic services for disturbed offenders, a general lock-up was imposed on the entire prison population. At that time the warden of the prison told the press:

> ... substantial evidence existed that the situation at the State Prison was rapidly deteriorating ... the issue was: would the staff control the institution or would chaos prevail. [*Concord Monitor,* March 21, 1973]

However, if the new "treatment team" thought that the "staff" included them, they were badly mistaken. During the 63-day lock-up, even those inmates in active treatment were denied the right to see any members of the team. It took weeks of negotiating with the warden *on the part of the chief psychiatrist* to see those inmates he felt were critical cases. In other words, when trouble occurred, not only were the inmates locked up but the "professionals" were locked out!

In all inmate disturbances, the staff had the universal reaction of dealing not with a disturbed psyche but a disturbed offender—that is, his actions, not his thoughts. Conflict and crisis in the maximum security prison revolve almost exclusively around the custodial function of the prison. The notion of the "non-routine situation" is anything that threatens physical security, and thus the group most relevant for this particular type of hazard are custodial officers. The final picture, then, of the "ideal" client is one who is a threat to the security of the institution and hence in need of control. Any conception of the inmate that runs counter to this prevailing one is automatically suspended in times of "real" crisis.

The "Emerging" Professional in the Prison

If the inmate suffers from the failures of practice, the guard suffers from the potential success of theory. Both are disturbed with the current reform movement. While the inmate is sure that "they" don't really mean it when "they" begin talking reform, the guard is afraid "they" really may. What is seen as a move forward by the former is seen as a clear threat by the latter. And in between is the warden or commissioner who must at the same time insist that he does and insist that he doesn't. The world may make liars of us all, but highly placed correctional officials seem particularly vulnerable.

One Commissioner of Corrections, for example, when quoted as finding "summary discipline" illegal and arbitrary, soon had a strike on his hands. Not a strike of inmates but of guards.[c] When one correctional officer in New England quit his post, he cited as his reasons the undercutting of prison "expertise" by the courts:

> The discipline is just being washed out completely. . . . You don't know where to move. You don't know how to move.[d]

Like so much else in the prison situation, normal social structure stands on its head. Far from being seen as a call for the "helping professions," which would acknowledge the inmate as a client in need of help, the crisis situation is defined as one requiring the *exclusive* attention of the custodians. Under "normal" conditions, the guards have indeed found much of their power circumscribed by court dictates. But precisely during crises—those non-routine situations that define the true structure of the profession and professional—the courts allow the prison official to move unilaterally, and in one direction. For example, a Federal Judge, when asked to end the New Hampshire lock-up, said:

> I am loath to interfere in the internal administration of the prison, particularly where the warden has made a decision that prison security was threatened and that an emergency existed. [*The Manchester Union Leader,* May 8, 1973.]

The courts have repeatedly told correctional personnel that their one source of competence is the control of the prison population. It is not surprising that, when guards strike, the predominate issue is who controls the prison.

> Howard Doyle, spokesman for the guards union . . . said a strike was likely because inmates were in control of the institution . . . the strike by guards (was) called to press their demand that they be given control of the prison. [*Concord Monitor,* March 15, 1973]

---

[c]Commissioner John O. Boone of Massachusetts, quoted in the *Concord Monitor,* August 13, 1972. Not surprisingly, Commissioner Boone has since been forced out of his position.

[d]From a statement given to the New Hampshire's Governor's Council, 1973.

In a system that provides the typical custodian with little professional image, the turn toward reducing him to a residual category cannot help but be seen as a personal threat. For it is clear enough that guards jealously guard—not only inmates but the expertise that this implies.

An example may suffice here. One guard at the New Hampshire Prison is in the habit of searching inmates "excessively" when they enter the visitor's room. We heard this complaint not from inmates but *from other guards*. He is seen as overly zealous and not very professional and is thus the butt of jokes made by his fellow custodians. The interesting feature of the guards' attitudes toward excessive searching is that since their professional competency occupies such an extremely narrow domain, any use of such techniques outside the non-routine or crisis situation tends to deflate the value of the few technqiues that comprise their claim to expert status.

As might be expected, many states are beginning to train guards to be "counselors" to inmates. In New Hampshire, treatment personnel wistfully talk of teaching guards behavior modification techniques! However, the prison is in a peculiar position that is a variant of what one author sees as a difficulty facing all newly-emerging professional groups:

> One of the most dramatic aspects of current social reform . . . [is]
> the struggle of newly emerging helping groups to establish their occu-
> pational identities. In the process, these groups often become trapped
> between their own promises to do good for their clients and their
> clients' disbelief or rejection of these occupational claims. [Fischer,
> 1969, Vol. 16, No. 4, pp. 423–433]

Equipped with training in psychology and sociology, the new "guard-counselor" faces situations that are pre-defined as calling for neither psychologists nor sociologists but simply guards. Insofar as these guards are called upon in the non-routine situations, the crises always involve their expertise as guards and thus their "real" clients are people who require surveillance and not necessarily counseling.

Inmates, of course, understand very well that the salient expertise of these new "guard-counselors" is still judged in terms of what constitutes a crisis *for the prison and not for themselves*. In short, they know that along this particular dimension they are not clients of counselors; at least in situations that represent crises—the very situations that determine professional standing—they are still inmates to be guarded and distrusted. When inmates at the Vermont State Prison in Windsor told us with regard to the new "counselors" that "a screw is still a screw," what they were noting is that they were still inmates.

Given that the typical crisis falls with the custodial function of the prison and hence organizational error entails guarding rather than providing services to inmates as clients, the prisoner is in a sense a mere necessary accessory to the operation of the prison. There is no structural change corresponding to the ideological shift in approaches to offenders. The relevant audience of the prison lies elsewhere.

De-Membering the Non-Member

If prisons are unique in their total lack of formal accounting procedures regarding the treatment of those nominally in their care, they are even more unique with regard to the *decision* as to the membership standing of the "participants." We will illustrate this by contrast to certain other service organizations.

All organizations have some test of membership. Even public agencies such as welfare, schools, and mental hospitals have minimal qualifying tests for admission to the services of that agency. In many cases, the will of the participant is taken for granted or even overruled. In this sense, a state mental hospital, a public school, and a prison cannot be distinguished. But even if the organization is not allowed to make judgments concerning who is a suitable member at the outset, there are almost universally accepted standards that the organization *itself* employs to decide when membership is to be terminated. This special privilege of controlling membership rests on three claims that are best exemplified by the organizational resources in medical care. However, variants of these claims can be found in all service organizations. These are that:

> ... there is an unusual degree of skill and knowledge involved in the professional work. ... Second, it is claimed that professions are responsible—that they may be trusted to work conscientiously without supervision. Third, the claim is that the profession itself may be trusted to undertake the proper regulatory action on those rare occasions when an individual does not perform his work completely or ethically. [Friedson, 1970, p. 137]

Until recently, a few procedural requirements were placed on schools when they decided to suspend or expel students. In the case of Madera vs. Board of Education of New York (1967), Judge Motley held that certain procedures of the board's review, which had led to expulsion, violated the due process clause of the 14th Amendment. Her ruling, however, did not affect the assumption that the board had the right and thus presumably the competency to regulate its membership. She was only concerned that particular procedures should be followed. Even that degree of outside control was mitigated when a circuit court *overruled* her judgment in the Madera case by asserting that:

> Law and order in the classroom should be the responsibility of our
> respective educational systems. The courts should not usurp this
> function. [Edwards, 1971, p. 14]

Whether or not a rule has been violated is ordinarily a matter of fact to be
determined by the school authorities. Unless they seriously abuse their discretion and act quite arbitrarily, a court will generally not review their decision.
In any case, while the choice involved in attending school up to a certain age
level is not a decision freely made, there is no law as yet that challenges the
principle that a board of education may suspend or expel from school any pupil
(or teacher) who for reasons of discipline (or competence) is being seriously
questioned.

The distinction between the claims of competency in prisons and other
organizations is made even sharper when considering the military. Here is
clearly a case where civil law can, in times of the draft, make participation
mandatory. Yet once that law is exercised, the rule of the military itself super-
sedes civil law. Many may be called but not necessarily chosen, and once
chosen not necessarily kept. It is quite clear that who decides the adequacy of
participation remains in the hands of the organization itself and not the agency
that first required participation.

While there are many cases concerning the credentials of proper members
in court-martial proceedings, none of them bear on the assumption that they
should be members of the same organization from which the deviant is to be
banned [Agcock and Wurfel, 1955]. And while Congress has provided for the
possibility of interservice eligibility to serve on a court-martial, in practice this
has been routinely defined by the services themselves as constituting procedural error [*Manual for Courts Martial*, 1951; see also U.S. vs. Catunolo (SP.
C.M. 405), 2 CMR 385, 386 (1952)].

In the case of civil commitment to mental hospitals, the argument still
obtains:

> Admission to a mental hospital has long implied the legal step of
> court commitment and detention; discharge on the other hand, has
> historically been left to doctors. . . . In general, medical considera-
> tions . . . determine when a patient may be released and whether
> his release and return to the community will be permanent and suc-
> cessful. [Special Committee to Study Commitment Procedures,
> 1962, p. 65]

New York statutes, however, provide for a special release committee of
three experienced psychiatrists to review problem cases being considered for
release. But, "The committee presents its written recommendations on release

to the director (of the hospital) *who makes the final determination*" [Special Committee . . ., 1962, p. 183].

What these examples amount to is that organizations—especially those within the service sector of the economy and thus restrained by highly articulated norms of practice—reserve for themselves the right to control their own membership or clientele. In part, the claim of expert status rests on this organizational resource—that is, as we noted at the outset of the chapter, organizations have as part of their necessary resources notions of what counts as their particular competency. Further, as noted, these competencies give rise to notions of what would constitute an error or mistake. Given that, organizational structures must include mechanisms for the control of error. Thus, if one of these competencies includes the management of membership in the organizations, members are free to note and complain if there appears to be a "mistake" in either the recruitment or dismissal of clientele. In the main, the organization then develops a review process in order to control such procedures and, of course, to legitimate them once they are challenged.

Determining the Indeterminate

While the prison is not the only place that receives its members from other agencies—and against the will of the members—it is the only institution that does not count as part of its organizational competency the special knowledge concerning the degree to which members either can or will benefit from its services. Neither does it claim the expertise required to dictate when those services will be terminated, i.e., when the inmate will be released. Further, as opposed to all other organizations, correctional officials themselves have *never* claimed this as an officially valid part of their professional mandate.

Historically, the legislatures in various states fixed definite penalties for each class of offenses. Coming directly on the heels of this change was the notion of rehabilitation (see Chapter 1). But there were inherent contradictions between these two reform movements shortly became clear:

[In the early period of the reform movement] rehabilitation was at odds with the stipulation that the criminal complete a predetermined and unalterable sentence. The sentencing regulations presented both inmates and officials with contradictory messages, but they easily learned which one to follow. On the one hand, the convict heard that the goal of confinement was reform and presumably wardens would judge him accordingly. . . . On the other hand, the prisoner knew a much more crucial fact—that he only had to endure a period of detention in order to be released. Officials could not arrange an early release for exemplary convicts or extend the confinement of recalcitrants. [Rothman, 1971, p. 250]

Yet as we argued earlier, these are essentially political and economic tensions. But the rush to psychologize such contradictions is not unique to the twentieth century:

> The New York Prison Commission of 1852 was among the first
> to argue that "protracted incarceration destroys the better faculties
> of the soul that most men who have been confined for long terms
> are distinguished by a stupor of both the moral and intellectual
> facilities. . . . Reformation is then out of the question." [Rothman, 1971, p. 244]

As early as 1787, Dr. Benjamin Rush urged the development of an indeterminate sentencing procedure to accompany changing parole regulations. When finally taken up by most jurisdictions, this remedy did more than merely move men out of prison quicker and under supervision. It added a decidedly new dimension to incarceration—that is, the length of imprisonment became a variable no longer in the hands of a legislative body that made decisions with regard to a class of *crime* but rather in the hands first of a judicial body and then of a paroling authority that made decision in terms of a class of *criminals.*

This shifting of both the terms of the decision as to the length of incarceration and the locus of such decision-making had the potential to hand prison officials a much more important power than they had wielded before—that is, who gets how much of what kind of treatment and for how long. Historically, this is a "burden" that these officials have taken pains to shed.

While parole boards were originally an integral part of the organizational structure of the prison, the movement over the last century has been to develop a parole system that is totally independent of the prison authorities. At the time of this writing, all states have either totally autonomous boards or boards that are within the department of corrections for administrative purposes only. Significantly, rather than jealously guarding a traditional organizational perogative—control of membership—the American Correctional Association has supported this trend. In its manual of correctional standards, the association has recommended that the board be in the department of corrections but not subordinate to it. *The effect of this recommendation is that the parole board be totally autonomous in terms of its decisional powers regarding the timing of inmate release.*

If the inmate's career through the prison system depends on his ability to demonstrate moral fitness, improvement, and acquiescence in decent societal standards of behavior, the Association of American Correctional Officers have apparently decided that they are not to be the one to pass judgment on the matter. This is no insignificant decision.

Like most prison reforms, the indeterminant sentence adds to rather than mediates the coercive function of the prison.

Bargaining In and Bargaining Out

Indeterminate sentence procedures with control located in a non-judicial body have deformalized the timing of the inmate's correctional career, have made the amount of time served dependent in some degree on his prison behavior, and have thus become a potential control device. But, as we have pointed out, prison officials have declined the opportunity of formally using this power themselves [*The Indeterminate Sentence,* 1954].[e] But surprisingly, that rejection of direct power results in benefits for the prison and losses for the inmate by truncating what has become a normal bargaining process in the criminal justice system.

Most cases before a criminal court are in fact end-products of an elaborate system of bargaining. Blumberg describes the process in the following way:

> The cop-out is in fact a charade, during which an accused must project an appropriate and acceptable degree of guilty, penitency and remorse. If he adequately feigns the role of the "guilty person" his hearers will engage in the fantasy that he is contrite and thereby merits a lesser plea. One of the essential functions of the criminal lawyer is that he coach his accused client in this performance. What is actually involved, therefore, is not a degradation or reinforcing process at all, but rather a highly structured system of exchange cloaked in the rituals of legalism and public professions of guilt and repentance. [Blumberg, 1964, p. 96]

The notion of the indeterminate sentence obviously entails that an inmate necessarily display the same amount of contriteness, moral resolve, and bargaining ability after as well as before sentencing. But, in effect, *there is no one to bargain with.* The inmate becomes an actor to an invisible audience while the warden serves as a mere messenger by relating the performance to a parole board. The only meaningful reviews can come from that invisible parole board, yet the only spectator with a seat is the warden.

While it was once true that an inmate would be released at a fixed date without regard for his behavior (short of outright mutiny), inmates are now essentially unaware just how long they will be behind bars.

Members of the prison staff are only too aware of the importance of time to the inmate. But rather than constraining prison officials, this fact merely provides them with a potential means for reinforcing the punitive aspects of prison by allowing officials to stress the amount of time an inmate may have to serve if he doesn't "measure up," while at the same time denying that the

---

[e]"In theory, the independent parole board is regarded as the best solution, and it may be said that the general tendency is to develop it. [Further] the American Prison Association recommends it." [The Indeterminate Sentence, 1954, p. 69]

same officialdom has any final say in the matter. It is another instance of control without accountability that we saw pervading penal life.

One inmate who was returned to prison on a parole violation was constantly kidded by guards who stressed that he would now have to serve a much longer period in prison. The inmate complained bitterly of the constant reminder. While able to raise the spectre of an increased sentence, the guards escaped the onus of the decision to enact the punishment. One is put in mind of children reminding a sibling that "Dad is really going to give it to you when he finds out what you've done," and then telling dad what he did.

If the officials with whom inmates come into regular contact are not empowered to make final decisions about release, then that appeal can be successfully denied—*minus the problems that are usually a result of such denials.* As one extremely high-placed corrections official said about the lack of control over the parole board's decision: "Let them make the mistakes. Anyway, then we don't have the inmates at us all the time.[f]

Although inmates complain about the warden's possible negative input into the parole decision, as long as these officials continue to disclaim as part of their expertise the ability to judge the membership of the prison, they are not accountable for decisions made in this regard.

One might be willing to trade off the unsettling psychological uncertainties involved in the indeterminant sentence for some real hope of a pay-off—a shorter sentence. But, as the following figures demonstrate, that pay-off is not only *not* forthcoming, it has been made even harder to obtain.

On a national basis in 1965, it was found that those inmates with determinate sentences spent a slightly shorter length of time in prison than those serving a more indeterminate sentence [U.S. Bureau of Prisons, 1965]. (Prisoners with definite sentences served slightly longer than those with indeterminate sentences only if prisoners serving life sentences are added into the first group. Even with this weighting, however, there is but the slightest of differences. The prisoners with definite sentences had a median time served figure of 17.3 months, while for those with indeterminate sentences the median was 16.4 months.) Jurisdictions such as California that specifically allow the total sentencing procedures—both minimum and maximum—to be handled by a non-judicial or legislative body kept their inmates in custody longer than those jurisdictions that maintained vestiges of the old minimum-maximum situation stipulated by legislatures.

---

[f]Compare this to the position of professionals in other settings. For example, Julius Roth tells us that in a hospital the conflict and bargaining over release is a major problem for both patients and physicians. "The physician faces a patient who is relatively well informed . . . a patient who frequently disagrees with the doctor's decision about when the treatment should end. The patient almost always wants to get out as soon as possible and frequently believes that the doctors are holding him longer than necessary." Roth goes on to devote a chapter to the bargaining processes that then ensue [Roth, 1968, chap. 3].

Studies in both California and New Hampshire indicate that length of time in correctional facilities in the case of the former is *independent* of whether or not the inmate will become a "repeater" [Select Committee on the Administration of Justice, 1970] but in the case of the latter *does predict* whether or not the inmate will suffer some psychological impairment. From the point of view of inmates or those seeking meaningful change, the "revolution" in sentencing procedures seems empty of both content and results.

Exiled from the Prison

We pointed out earlier that a constant factor across all organizations is the ability to regulate its membership. Given that the prison at least formally is unable to regulate its own membership, one would expect other forms of regulation to arise. Like many states that operate more than one correctional facility, the maximum security facility in Vermont has become a "dumping ground"[g] for those inmates who are felt to be unfit for the less custodial-minded Community Correctional Centers. As one official of the maximum security facility in Windsor, Vermont, told us: "They should take the sign down from the state insane asylum and put it up over the doors of the prison here."

Indeed, one's impression of the inmates (or "residents" as they are euphemistically referred to by the Department of Corrections) at the Windsor facility is that they are more disturbed than those found in other maximum security facilities that hold all of the convicted felons in the state. However, what is unclear is the cause and effect relationship between the use of the facility and the kind of inmate found it it.

The group of men at Windsor fall mainly into three categories: those who have a long sentence because of a serious crime; those who have been disciplinary problems at the correctional centers, and those deemed non-rehabilitative for one reason or another by a classification committee. Approximately a quarter of the men at Windsor started out their prison careers assigned to a correctional center and were subsequently transferred to the maximum security facility.

While these categories appear clear-cut, quite often the decision to transfer a man entails all three. Further, the records of the men transferred to the maximum security prison clearly indicate that the use of the facility was "multipurpose." For example, a 23-year-old inmate was recommended by the court during his trial to a Community Correctional Center. But the classification committee thought otherwise. The following excerpt from the inmate's record justifies his spending the greater part of his sentence at the "dumping ground":

---

[g]This was the description given to the Windsor facility by one of its officials. Attica was also considered by New York inmates and officers as a dumping ground, and it was the practice to send both parole violators and "aggressive" inmates to that facility.

(The court's recommendation) could not be realistically implemented
(on the basis of) the following facts. (1) Long minimum sentence.
(2) The individual's lack of commitment to rehabilitation. (3) His
need to develop at least minimal anxiety in a more abrasive setting
which will thus provide the possibility of successful intervention.

On the other hand, another inmate went to the "more abrasive setting"
because of a sentence the classification committee believed was too short:

We see no chance of success on probation. . . . Punitive measures
alone cannot possibly help him . . . program which comes closest to
meeting his needs is that of the treatment unit at this facility (a
Community Correctional Center) . . . long-term exposure will be
required. The maximum possible sentence for his present offense
would be totally inadequate.

The classification committee does not note what will happen when this
last inmate develops the "minimal anxiety" that they predict for a former
inmate who, once he develops it, will be led to a Community Correctional
Center for "intervention."

For most of the inmates, however, transferral to the maximum security
facility was a "disciplinary" measure. For example, one transfer order reads:

[The inmate] was involved in some rather serious actions resulting in
disciplinary hearing during this stay at the . . . community correctional
center. These actions on his part . . . played a role in the final decision for transfer to Windsor.

The result is an institution that can have no clear-cut mandate since its
population ranges from young political activists to extremely disturbed older
inmates—that is, short-term inmates who would probably not be in the correctional system long enough to be "treated" and inmates with very long sentences
who would be in the system long enough to wait for their turns at community
correctional centers all found their way to Windsor.

Simultaneously, then, the same setting is used to promote a psychological
state that will prepare a man for further "treatment" to provide a holding
action because nothing much could be done for another man, and to serve as
a specific punishment for a third man. While the reasons bringing a man to
the maximum security facility may vary widely, there is nothing in the institution's structure to allow for a parallel differentiation in their treatment.

Given the tendency to define problems within the structural and technical
capabilities at hand, incarceration literally becomes a holding action. The
expertise of the staff is reduced to the custodial level, despite whatever good
reform intentions there may be for the maximum security facility represents

the end of the line to both the department and the inmate. Any behavior that is out of bounds is also outside the organizational remedies of the staff of that facility. Once the inmate reaches the maximum security institution in multi-facility states, the character of the work for officials and staff changes drama-tically. The change consists in their inability to define problems that are outside the scope of that institution since nothing is left to be accomplished. Thus, by structural definition, these inmates become the "incorrigibles" with whom the facility is prepared to deal. This idea does not violate the notion that "profes-sionals" have a mandate "to define whether or not a problem exists and what the 'real' character of that problem is and how it should be managed" [Freid-son, 1970, p. 303], for, in fact, it is just this feature of "professionalism" that produces the effects described here. Given the *structural* limitations on what kind of expertise is possible, prison staffs come to define in professional terms and thus develop a stake in the "incorrigible" character of their charges.

In states where all convicted felons go to the *same* facility, the problem of getting rid of a "member" is, of course, more severe. In New Hampshire, which we can take to be representative of such states, the typical strategies have been to isolate the inmate through various degrees of segregation. On the other hand, courts have become ready to claim that such procedures must follow very par-ticular guidelines. But, as we have argued, the staff feels such pressure from the court as an usurpation of their traditional role in the prison and thus have re-sorted to other mechanisms to "exile" the "exiled." One of the more usual moves is to send the inmate to the state mental hospital.

In 1972, 6,190 inmates in the various penitentiaries in America were trans-ferred to state mental hospitals.[h] This represents roughly 6 percent of the total inmate population and 3 times the national average for psychiatric admissions for that year. During our tenure at the New Hampshire State Prison, fully 10 percent of the inmates had been transferred at least once to the state hospital.

This method of exiling the prisoner has still to be reviewed precisely by the courts because, as Barbara Wooten, points out, it appears to be in the name of science rather than punishment.

> Without question . . . in the contemporary attitude toward antisocial
> behavior, psychiatry and humanitarianism have marched hand in hand.
> Just because it is so much in keeping with the mental atmosphere of a
> scientifically-minded age, the medical treatment of social deviants has
> been a most powerful, perhaps even the most powerful, reinforcement
> of humanitarian impulses; for today the prestige of humane proposals
> is immensely enhanced if these are expressed in the idiom of medical
> science. [Wooten, 1959, p. 206]

---

[h]Information provided by the National Institute for Mental Health in advance of forthcoming publication.

What Wooten claims for humanitarian instincts is also true for the felt need of prison personnel to control their institutions. Couched in the idiom of medical science, such control methods escape unnoticed both by the courts and at times the inmates themselves. The maximum security wing at the New Hampshire Hospital would not fit anyone's idea of a humanitarian impulse. If psychiatry has "used the legal powers of the state in the accomplishment of its goals" [Zola, 1972, pp. 487–504], the state, in the form of the prison, has most certainly used psychiatry to accomplish *its* goals. As one psychiatrist specializing in penal work points out, when an inmate fails to respond to punishment in what the prison officials conceive of as a normal fashion, transferring out of the system via the state mental hospital becomes the only viable alternative [Halleck, 1967].

The question is, are these inmates in need of hospitalization? It is difficult to argue the question since by definition hospitalization is a "cultural" product requiring definitions of behavior as the kind that should be "treated." If we live in a culture where crime is seen as sickness, then clearly all inmates should be in a hospital. But, of course, that is not what one is really after. The question is, are they emotionally disturbed by "normal" standards? Research by criminologists Harry E. Barnes and Negley K. Teeters led to the following conclusion:

> The bulk of our criminals are not emotionally disturbed. In general it would seem reasonable to assume that a cross-section of the criminal world would show no more emotional imbalance that could be found in the general population. [Barnes and Teeters, 1959, p. 7]

Furthermore, *the diagnosis of mental illness is no clear guarantee that psychiatric treatment will be forthcoming.*

Due to a peculiarity in the New Hampshire law this last point can be shown most graphically. The statutes governing the commitment of those *acquitted* of criminal charges by reason of insanity permits the judge to send such individuals to the *prison*!

> ... the court, if it is of opinion that it will be dangerous that such person should go at large, may commit him to the prison or to state hospital for life until or unless earlier discharged, released, or transferred by due course of law. [New Hampshire Revised Statutes, Ann. 607:3 (Supp. 1972)]

At the time of this writing, 5 of the inmates at the New Hampshire State Prison were there by virtue of this commitment procedure. In other words, state psychiatrists have declared them legally insane. Yet once in the prison none of these inmates were treated for the supposed psychiatric ailments that caused them ostensibly to be defined as insane. When any of them finally did see a psychiatrist, it was only after some disruptive behavior in the prison.

One inmate who was acquitted on grounds of insanity is perhaps typical of the use of psychiatry in the prison. After having been adjudicated as insane he was not referred to a therapist during the first 4 months of his incarceration; referral came at his own request, when he told the prison nurse that he "was at the breaking point."[i] The therapist ultimately saw the inmate and entered the following notes:

> On the basis of interview and [the state hospital diagnosis] I believe he is not mentally ill. Cannot be helped by prison. May be detrimental. Besides proper treatment facilities are at [the state hospital] and should be transferred.

As of this writing, this man was still at the prison and has yet to see the inside of the hospital or enter any type of treatment on a regular basis with a therapist. After the second and last time this inmate saw a therapist, the sole note that appears on his record is "symptoms of depression"!

Of the 5 inmates adjudicated as insane but living among the general prison population, the one who *did* see the inside of the state mental hospital displays the typical pattern that follows commitment to prison rather than to a medical facility. Although he had been found insane, the inmate received no psychiatric or any other therapeutic services for the first 5 months of his incarceration. However, once he became disruptive in the prison, he literally bounced back and forth between the state hospital and the prison, over 7 times in a 2-year period. Yet, in all of the time he was in the hospital, only 5 notes from the psychiatrist who treated him could be located in the man's records. In each case, the notations refer only to orders for medication for "anxiety and nervousness."

Far from the hospital being used for therapeutic intent, it is a device to "cool-out" those whom the prison is incapable of exiling in any other fashion. However, the device is short-lived since it is outside the control of prison authorities—that is, once the inmate is received at the hospital, it is then up to the superintendent of that facility to decide whether or not he will keep the patient (inmate). The average stay of the inmate at the New Hampshire hospital is approximately one-quarter that of patients in state facilities nationally.

As one inmate who has had extensive experiences with short stays at the hospital told us: "They zonk you at the hospital with drugs and send your

---

[i]It is not surprising that inmates are forced to extreme acts, whether they be of an overt, potentially violent nature or of a suicidal, "breaking point" nature in order to receive even minimal attention. Their situation, as we have pointed out, is an intimate part of the situation facing those with little money, no direct political clout, and little status in our society.

body back here where the state said it had to be. Nobody gives a damn where your head is. The only way to make it is then stay zonked on your own or get it from the doc. Either way half of the guys in here are out of it all the time."

The pattern of the use of the hospital that can be found in various inmates' files corroborates this account. One inmate, for example, was accused of threatening to take the door off his cell (a remarkable feat). Two days later the records merely note that he was sent to the state hospital. After 6 days the records indicate he was returned to the prison. The following are the only doctor's notes on the case:

> After admitted given large dosages of thoarazine at first involuntarily followed by oral stalzine during the day and thorizine at night. Delusions of persecution and violent threats disappear. Past three days better while on Prolixim 24 mg. I.M. every two weeks. Ready for return.

Illness has long been treated as a legitimated exemption from normal role obligations in sociological literature. However, little attention has been paid to the fact that illness can also be used by institutions to exempt parts of their membership. If people use poor health to legitimize a sense of failure, it can be said that prisons use the poor mental health of its population to legitimize that which they are *organizationally* constrained from doing. And that is controlling their membership—still, however, without the usual review procedures that such overt control would normally imply.

Since transferring inmates to a mental hospital facility brings in judgments that are rendered by non-penal personnel and thus are controlled by alien ideas of who is and who is not a candidate for such transfers, penal personnel often resort to transfer *within* the correctional system.

For states such as New York or California, this has generally been done with ease since these jurisdictions operate more than one maximum security facility. On the other hand, in states having but one penitentiary, the problem can become acute. The New England states have solved this problem by entering into what is called the New England Compact whereby states agree to receive each other's inmates who can not be successfully integrated into their own state penitentiary. That such inmates are in a sense essentially exiles can be seen by noting one experience we had in interviewing inmates in New Hampshire.

We inadvertently asked to see an inmate who had been transferred to the New Hampshire facility from Maine. When the warden discovered we had interviewed this "outsider," he told us that we shouldn't have: "He isn't one of ours, we're just holding him for Maine."

This holding action is not unique. In 1965, almost half of all inmates in correctional facilities in this country were there not by original court order but by administrative transfer. This represents an increase over a 15-year period of 90 percent [U.S. Bureau of Prisons, 1965].

While penal custodians have disclaimed the responsibility for deciding who gets out of prison *in general,* they have grasped a functional equivalent for controlling their *own* specific membership. This is hardly explicable as a response to increasing professional competency (no matter how many of those transfers may be disguised in medical jargon), but can be viewed simply as a result of increased court surveillance of the more "primitive" exiling methods.

In these two decades, the courts have begun to rule that both the due process clause and the clause restricting cruel and unusual punishment pertain to inmates not only prior to but *during* incarceration. With this legal recognition, inmates have increasingly filed writs asking for redress of practices that, in their intent and result, had isolated the inmate from the general prison population. As one well-placed prison official in Vermont confided in this regard: "The inmates think they have the department of corrections on the run. And, let's face it, they do!"

Generally escaping judicial notice, however, has been the practice of simply sending the inmate to a sister institution. Transfer has become a more expedient means of controlling institutional membership since it (1) does not usually come under judicial review, and (2) does not appear concretely as an exercise of punishment. This system of transferring recalcitrant inmates is not without its small ironies, one of which concerns the practice in federal prisons of "bussing." An inmate from New Hampshire was transferred in March to Lewisburg, Pennsylvania. By June he had been in 4 federal institutions; from Pennsylvania, immediately after the initial period of "quarantine," this inmate was sent to Terra Haute, Indiana; Leavenworth, Kansas; and El Reno, Oklahoma, before being returned to New Hampshire. Testifying before a federal judge, he said that at each prison except Leavenworth "they threw me in the hole, isolation." At Leavenworth, he said, "They were going to throw me in the hole but they couldn't because the hole was full" [*Concord Monitor,* June 20, 1973].

Conclusion

We have discussed the uniqueness of prisons in terms of the peculiar status arrangements of its "members" as compared to other "treatment" organizations as well as its unique refusal to take *official* responsibility for them. This state of affairs obviously heightens tensions among an already tense population. While the inmate may well have many concrete "demons," he will find that in the long run his real confrontation is with a "ghost." The organizational structure of the prison precludes most inmates from gaining *institutional* knowledge for the *image* of stability—represented by the strictly punitive, one-man rule of traditional prisons—has changed.

No longer are the custodians guards, but counselors with specialized training. No longer does the legislature or individual judge decide the degree or kind of punishment. Instead, a pretrial classification team of experts mulls over various "factors," the defense lawyer, prosecuting attorney, and judge make informal, effectively invisible decisions concerning the court plea, and an independent, floating parole board makes final decisions about release. No longer does the warden decide that a man should be placed in solitary, but that he should be "treated." And this decision rests putatively on the shoulders of therapists, vocational rehabilitation experts, and social workers. In short, the approach toward inmates is now "scientized" so that punishment is no longer punishment, but behavior modification; no longer incarceration but, as in Vermont, "aversion therapy."

Nonetheless, there is no positive indication that inmates are now treated significantly different than if "top management" were left alone with key decision along the traditional punishment mode. While the claims for what is being done to and for the inmate have changed, the system of accountability within which prisons must operate as an on-going social organization remains constant. What the prisons cannot do in the name of punishment, they are only too free to do in the name of science. Obviously, it cannot matter much to the inmate whether a committee keeps him in a more "abrasive setting" so as to "facilitate future rehabilitation" or whether he is simply sent to the hole.

The onus of responsibility for what is essentially dirty work is now spread out among experts and neutralized in the name of science. While masking itself with the respectable facade of modern organizations, the prison encapsulates none of the control mechanisms that such organizations claim, and thus none of their vulnerability in the face of mistakes. Prisons don't make mistakes.

5 The Lawful Prison

The reason the prison has never developed structural arrangements that adequately correspond to a treatment model is precisely because what the inmate is *now* claimed to suffer from was never a disease. Crime is a failure to obey the law; nothing more, nothing less. To raise that behavior to the level of a pathology is to alter radically what we understand the law to be. That this is so should come as no surprise since laws are the highest expression of the state, and the role of the state has been transformed. As we argued earlier, the penitentiary was a response to the needs of a market society. But such a society has long since disappeared and has been replaced by what Kolko [1963, p. 3] has called "political capitalism" that consists in. . . the utilization of political outlets to attain conditions of stability, predictability and security—to attain rationalization—in the economy." That this tendency corresponds to the same program as that of political liberals is of some interest. "The changes in the concept of the proper role of government and in the techniques of maintaining political and social stability reflected the end of "free" competition and the rise of a new corporate oligarchy. In the rhetoric of the new liberals, these concepts represented a growing concern for the welfare of the public (and many ordinary liberals and probably some corporate liberals were so motivated)" [Weinstein, 1969, p. 252].

In the market society the function of the state was to protect capitalists from one another and from the aristocracy; the state was an impersonal legal structure that merely maintained a neutral position between competing interests. The best government, it was held, governed least. But unrestrained competition, growing complexity of the system itself and the real fear of dwindling profits from contracting markets led to a very different view of government. The *accomplishment* of the rational liberal state provided the conditions whereby the state can, through bureaucratic, administrative and, above all, *legal* channels control

> . . . the destructive potential of growing competition and the danger-ous possibilities of a formal political democracy that might lead to a radical alteration of the distribution of wealth or even its total expro-priation. [Kolko, 1963, p. 302]

Thus, beginning in the early part of this century, business increasingly turned to federal legislation to accomplish what it could not do for itself

[Kolko, 1963, p. 2]. Rather than the corporate state being lawless, it has
become increasingly lawful. This is simply to argue that the "form" within
which things get done is increasingly worked out within a legal structure that,
by its very existence, acclaims whatever is done is right. (For a fuller exposition
of this position, see Weber [1967].)

The law itself now represents the "interests of the economic elites who
control the production and distribution of the major resources of the society"
[Chambliss, 1973, p. 430].[a] But in order to do so, the law must take on a
value that is quite apart from the contents of any specific piece of legislation;
the law becomes a surrogate of any personally derived morality [Chambliss,
1973, p. 453]. "It does so by supplying the sole normative standard in a
society." Where the liberal state began in a separation of ethics from the law,
it ends with the *identification* of the former with the latter. This law of rules
supplied by a "disinterested" government is naturally replicated in its prisons.
O'Neill states this nicely:

> A political community has always to find a symbolic expression of
> its beliefs concerning the sources, mechanisms and threats to the
> orderly relationships between its members. The symbolism of the
> body politic is a recurring expression of the nature of order and
> disorder in the political community. [O'Neill, 1972, p. 68]

Prisons, above all else, symbolize the law-like nature of the state and the lawless nature of its inmates. This feature of prisons interfaces with the need to
treat inmates within a model that claims that it is both "humane" and "helpful" to deprive a person of his liberty on the grounds that he is incapable of
following rules and that imprisonment will restore this ability.

Each of these characteristics of the modern prison, therefore, must be
played out in little "rituals" that affirm the nature of prisons and the assumptions upon which they are based.[b] A chief source of these rituals are the various
formal procedures characteristic of all maximum security prisons and increasingly a product of statutory rules—the disciplinary hearing.

------

[a]"Conventional myths notwithstanding, the history of the criminal law is not an history
of public opinion or public interest being reflected in criminal law legislation. On the contrary,
the history of the criminal law is everywhere the history of legislation and appellate court
decisions which in effect (if not in intent) reflect the interests of the economic elites" [Cham-
bliss, 1973, p. 430].

[b]What follows is heavily dependent on the insights of Irving Goffman [1961, p. 87].
However, what we are proposing is that his analysis is incomplete without providing an
analysis of the contemporary social, political, and economic setting. For example, his statement, "total institutions can little afford . . . determinism. Inmates must be caused to self-
direct themselves in a manageable way . . . ," we take to be true, but not invariant, and tied
into the logic of the political and economic community with which the institution must
interact and to which it must be responsive.

Punishing the Punished

Prison administrators have traditionally claimed the right of "procuring conformity of inmates to the behavior patterns required of them for the smooth functioning of institutions" [Glaser, 1972, p. 329]. Historically, the means used in that quest have provided material for much of the scandal surrounding prison management. In the name of discipline, methods were often used that had long been banned from use in the name of punishment. Today, discipline is claimed to be an integral part of the reform process itself, "augmenting the rehabilitative influences of inmate staff relationships" [Glaser, 1972, p. 33].

Regardless of the overt concern in such procedures—whether it be for smooth sailing or rehabilitation—the ritual surrounding disciplinary hearings is as important as the actual instrumental control it provides. On each and every occasion, no matter what the ostensible content of these hearings, their main business will be to assert the primacy of rules and the fundamental nature of the inmate as someone deficient in his ability to follow them.

Jones appeared before a disciplinary committee charged with being disrespectful to an officer. He had called the officer a "pig-mother-fucker" after being told to remove a blanket that covered his cell door and prevented visional access by those in the corridor. Jones was not charged with hanging up his blanket, for, as attested to by members of the disciplinary board, there were no posted regulations covering such cases. While there was no rule against the behavior that precipitated the dispute between the guard and Jones, there most certainly was a rule about Jones not entering into disputes with guards. Of course, Jones received 5 days' lock-up in his cell for his infraction.

What lesson is Jones to learn from all of this? First of all, he must learn that a commitment to a course of action—in this case gaining some warmth by preventing cold air from entering the unprotected bars of his cell door—is always reversible in the face of rules to the contrary—that is, the universe of behaviors that can be successfully covered by rules is necessarily finite and is provided for by creating the omnipotent rule concerning the relationship that must obtain between officer and inmate. Jones' real commitment must be to "rules" rather than to his own needs, or rather his own needs must be worked out within the rules. Joining the two together is apparently an everyday feature of life outside of prison as well. However, in prison there is a special feature that undermines the very function of rule-following behavior, which is ostensibly sought by the disciplinary hearings and which adds to the lessons Jones must learn.

As Goffman points out, commitment to the rules is displayed by the actor in arranging to remove himself from the physical circumstances that would make non-adherence profitable [Goffman, 1969]. It is as much the voluntary removal on the part of the actor as it is the physical fact of removal that gives evidence of his commitment to a course of action to other parties involved in the interaction. In prison, however, commitment can never be displayed in such a fashion simply because there is always the open question of whether anything whatsoever is done voluntarily.

The commitment to rules is an observable phenomenon to other interested parties precisely because the actor has a series of choices. In the absence of choice there arises some doubt concerning the depth of commitment, its sincerity, and thus the certainty that the commitment is real. Without this kind of resource, which makes commitment apparent, the inmate can be seen and in turn treated as a pretty slippery character when it comes to abiding by rules, he may follow them at any given moment, but there is no betting on his doing so in the future.

This feature of prisons explains both the prevalence and use of disciplinary hearings. The hearings themselves display the assumption that inmates are those kinds of people who cannot or will not commit themselves to rules, and thus publicly "reveal" the fundamental nature of the people with whom they must deal. In so doing they are like ceremonies that catch our attention, divert it from features of the prison, and center it instead, on features of the individual inmate. But this is not enough; there is an end to the drama that the observer almost always knows in advance—the hearings are settings in which the inmate is almost always shown to be guilty of some rule infraction.

The Rule of Law in Prisons

Some have held that the prison is in fact a display of lawlessness being corrected by "the gradual entry in some areas of the rule of law" [Mitford, 1973, p. 248]. By the judicial change in the "hands-off policy" regarding administrative matters in prisons, it is suggested that conditions will improve [Mitford, 1973, ch. 14]. While this may be true in the short run, it would be wholly deceptive to look to the intervention of the legal system of the larger community to protect the imprisoned. For legal safeguards depend on the context within which they work. If, as in the prison, the context is inappropriate to the laws involved, one is left with vacuous formalities—that is, not lawlessness, but empty laws. As Anatole France wryly put it some years back:

> The law in its majesty, equally forbids rich and poor alike from
> sleeping under bridges, stealing bread and begging in the streets.

The courts have held that disciplinary hearings must follow due process, as evidenced by a number of cases that hold that due process is a relevant procedural safeguard within prisons. The following from Sostre vs. McGinnis 442 F. 2d 178 (2d Cir. 1971) contains the basic premise that is generally used in current litigation: ". . . our constitutional scheme does not contemplate that society may commit lawbreakers to the caprious and arbitrary actions of prison officials." While this does not preclude the possibility of defendants being found guilty, it certainly does indicate the opposite possibility. But this possibility—even with all available legal safeguards—is almost totally absent from such hearings. And there are good reasons why this situation cannot be adequately addressed by legal safeguards.

Two facts of prison life both "explain" the high rate of guilty verdicts and militate against assuming that the hearings serve an exclusive purpose of acting as a material control on the smooth running of the prison. First, and most important, most infractions are of rules that have absolutely no bearing on what would be considered "criminal" in the larger community but instead are oriented to displays of conformity within the prison. In a survey of one maximum security institution, we found that 89 percent of all disciplinary charges placed against the inmates were for administrative infractions rather than infraction of rules that would have caused criminal proceedings in the outside world.

Secondly, the smooth running of the institution seems to be as much tied to notions of etiquette appropriate to mid-Victorian ladies as to any need of the institution. For example, a significant number of rules in most prisons cover the inmate's appearance. In New Hampshire, the length of one's hair was an issue that caused many inmates to be brought up before the disciplinary committee. In one instance, a young inmate spent months in the "annex" (the unit reserved for dealing with disciplinary problems) for refusing to cut his hair. Prison regulations in most institutions seem to be as concerned with the clothing of inmates as *Vogue or Women's Wear Daily*; there are lists of the kinds of clothes that can be worn and, in the case of one institution, how those clothes can be pressed and tailored![c]

Given these two characteristics of the rules and their enforcement in the prison—that most rule infractions are of the administrative variety and that administrative rules appear almost caprious with regard to the "smooth" functioning of the institution—it can be expected that not only will inmates be "found" guilty but that these hearings are explicable in terms of their function of providing a subtle means of ratifying the social reality of the prison, the absence of which would call into question the legitimacy of what is being done to the convict.[d]

By accepting at face value strict notions of the legalistic nature rather than

---

[c]There are few cases concerning rights to dress as one pleases and those which have been decided with regard to hair length generally uphold the power of prison officials to determine length and cut of hair [cf. Books vs. Wainwright 428 f2d 652 (5th Cir. 1970)].

[d]"If an organization must have security in its environment, then certainly [the] observation that too much security can be stultifying and corrosive is at least well taken." Organizations have "a need for a moderate challenge or threat" [Gouldner, 1955, pp. 496–507]. Ironically, in the case of prisons their organizational security is *only* provided by obvious threat [cf. ch. IV].

the performative character of his hearings, the prisoner can be made to look absurd. Inmate F.......... was being "tried" for refusing to submit to a strip search. In accordance with the legal guidelines established for such performances, he asked for a 7-day continuance to better prepare his case. This routine plea, provided for by the legalistic model of the performance, was simply ignored. The counselor (a social worker employed by the prison) and the inmate discussed the matter in an adjoining room. The topic at hand, however, was apparently *not* the continuance. For all that could be overheard was the counselor berating the prison inmate for taking him away from an important budgetary meeting. Upon re-entering the room, the counselor asked the man in charge of the hearing a few short questions:

> *Counselor*: "Is there a difference between a shake-down and a
>   search?"
> *Man in charge*: "Why, yes, of course."
> *Counselor*: "Is this a customary part of routine?"
> *Man in charge*: "Yes, it is."
> *Counselor*: "Was he the only one?"
> *Man in charge*: "No, there were nine [who refused to submit to
>   searches] that day."
> *Inmate* (interrupting angrily): "If one officer is going to make you
>   strip they all should!"

Nobody said a word. The inmate repeated his complaint. Much of the paper on the table was in need of reshuffling and that took some time. While this was occurring, the counselor changed roles and "counseled" the inmate to plead guilty. "After all," he reasoned, "you did break a rule." This clearly confused the inmate, as such public statements turn the presumption of innocence, so critical to the legalistic model, on its head. This marked the beginning of a series of increasingly shorter outside conferences between inmate and counselor, during which those remaining in the hearing room made a variety of jokes about the silliness being displayed by the inmate.

The reality that the inmate and his keepers reside in two very different moral universes was never more apparent. And within the separate universe of the inmate was his confusion about the status of the legal model upon which he was basing his entire defense. Although the situation was predefined for him as being "by the book," the "book" was proving impossible to locate. The intervention of the legal system of the larger community was there only as a theoretical shadow. It did the inmate no good and had the result of making all his efforts appear desperate, stupid, and even absurd.

He finally said that on advice of his counselor he was dropping his request for a continuance. He was found guilty and given a punishment of 10 days without visitations except by a member of the cloth or the bar.

The performance, then, should be looked at not only in terms of what it claims is going on but in terms of what the upshot of the performance itself is. In short, each and every aspect of the hearings, while ostensibly devoted to "getting at the truth" and "deciding the proper penality," are simultaneously staging what must be upheld as the truth about those engaged in the performance.

For example, though it was considered a step forward to allow inmates to testify in their own behalf when brought up on disciplinary charges [Cluchette vs. Procunier, 328 F. Supp. 767 (N.D. Cal., 1971)], such a reform abets rather than diminishes the effect of the hearings. For social conditions—conditions that the community hold out to be true of individuals—depict the degree of confidence that can be placed in their testimony, irrespective of the presence of legal safeguards.

> The credibility of a witness may be impeached on the following grounds: (a) by showing his general bad reputation; (b) by questioning him on cross examination concerning any immoral, vicious, or criminal acts allegedly committed by him, which may affect his character and tend to show he is not worthy of belief; (c) by showing that he has been convicted of a crime. [Fisher, 1961, p. 108][e]

What inmate could possibly pass the test? On each and every count his words are open to doubt, not because the events he depicts are implausible but because of a social role that necessarily testifies to his being one whose word is open to serious question. The hearings themselves provide the social mechanisms that repeatedly make salient the unsavory characteristics of inmates. The hearings dramatize repeatedly the faulty material with which the prison officials must deal.

In every type of hearing, from those which involve infractions of purely administrative rules to those that would result in revocation of parole [Morissey vs. Brewer, 443 F. 2d 942 (1972)], courts are insisting on the relevance of the due process clause of the Fourteenth Amendment. But the clause does not abrogate the very social situation within which the inmate finds himself and which can only add to the dramatic quality of his inevitable denouncement.

Under the due process clause, for example, the courts have held that inmates have a right to call witnesses to testify on behalf of the accused [Cluchette vs. Procunier, 328 F. Supp. 767 (N.D. Cal., 1971)] Two features of the prison situation, however, not only reduce the "safeguard" intention of such orders but add to the effect of the proceedings to which we are referring. First, by virtue of the radical polarization of the prison population—one is either staff or inmate—there is little probability that a member of the staff will testify on

---

[e]Quoted in Goffman [1969, pp. 125–126].

the inmate's behalf. (While he may testify as to mitigating circumstances, he will not challenge the word of a fellow member of the staff without fear of either losing his job or at least spending some very uncomfortable moments with colleagues.) Therefore, the inmate has no recourse but to call as witnesses fellow inmates who themselves are as suspect as the accused.

There is no disputing that the disciplinary hearings, regardless of intent, serve as little ceremonies that publicly display the necessity of educating the inmate to the importance of adhering to "rules." Even the American Correctional Association asserts the educative function of disciplinary hearings:

> Discipline . . . looks beyond the limits of the inmate's terms of confinement. It must seek to insure carry-over value by inculcating standards which the inmate will maintain after release. It is not merely the person's ability and desire to conform to institutional rules and regulations but his ability and desire to conform to accepted standards for individuals and community life in free society. [*Manual of Correctional Standards*, 1966, pp. 3-19]

The invocation of due process and other legal safeguards—far from reducing the ceremonial aspect that symbolizes the nature of the threat that inmates represent—ratify the message these rituals are intended to convey by conferring legitimacy to them.

Disciplinary functions of the prison allow an objective manifestation of the conditions that the doctrine of the modern penal system holds to be true. There are two polarized avenues available for the rebellious inmate in response to this. The first takes the law at its word and temporarily transforms the inmate into a pedantic, legalistic Philadelphia lawyer. Such was the case with inmate N.......... who was also being tried for refusal to submit to a strip search.

He sat down in the hearing room, nodded as his rights were recited to him, and addressed the hearing board: "In all honesty, I want to know if any of you have made up your minds about the case. I want to know if you have already found me guilty or not." The presiding officer responded: "Of course not. We haven't heard the testimony and have not yet deliberated about the merits of the case."

The inmate began his presentation by pointing out that when the officer demanded that he take his clothes off he had not refused; he had only refused to strip *himself*. If the officer wanted to perform the act, that would have been perfectly satisfactory, but the *officer* had refused. The proceedings continued with the following exchanges:

> *Inmate*: "Why should I remove clothes on my body and not you?"
> *Guard*: "That's common procedure."
> *Inmate*: "Instituted by whom?"
> *Guard*: "I don't know."

(There was some discussion between members of the board to determine who in fact instituted such orders. The name of the superior
officer was found and entered into the record.)

Inmate: "Did I or did I not say you could do it for me?"
Guard: "Yes, you did, but it's common knowledge that the inmate
    strips himself."
Inmate: "Well, I didn't know that. Would it be natural for a man
    to remove his own clothing?"
Guard: "I don't know."
Inmate: "How would a cop on the street strip and search a suspect?"
Guard: "I don't know. I'm not a cop."
Parole Officer: "What is common procedure in these cases?"
Inmate: "Did you . . ."
Parole Officer: "I'd like to know what is common procedure here."
Inmate: "Did you hear me *refuse* to be strip-searched?"
Man in Charge: "Yes, this is common procedure."
Guard: "No."
Inmate: "I draw your attention to the fact that there is absolutely
    nothing in the posted regulations concerning *who* does the
    stripping. All it says is that the guard has the right to inspect
    the inmate, not who does it."

(A second guard was then brought in and the inmate began question-
ing him.)

Inmate: "Of your own knowledge did you hear me refuse to be
    searched?"
Guard: "No."
Man in Charge: "Now, isn't it the case . . ."
Inmate: "Excuse me, sir, but this is my witness. And I have no
    further questions for him at this time."
Parole Officer: "I think my question has not been answered. I've
    been trying to find out if it's normal procedure for the guard
    to strip the inmate or the other way around. I mean, is it nor-
    mal procedure for . . ."
Man in Charge: "It's normal procedure for the inmate to take his
    clothes off by himself. The guards don't do that."
Inmate (lifting up a large, dog-eared legal textbook): "I draw your
    attention to a recent statute in the California District Court . . ."
Man in Charge: "I'm familiar with that law."
Inmate: "Well, it clearly states that . . ."
Man in Charge: "I know what it states. But this is not that district.
    We are not in California and that doesn't apply here."

(At this point the inmate conferred briefly for the first time with his
    case counselor. Then he made his final appeal.)

Inmate: "The word 'normal' keeps popping up here. But taking clothes off is abnormal in or out of jail. The strip search is so inconsistent, many times I have not been searched. The regulation bulletin is not at all specific with regard to who does the stripping. When the criteria are vague, it should be resolved in my favor. Thank you."

(With that he left the room, accompanied by two correctional officers and a legal textbook.)

Man from State Department of Corrections: "He's sprung a lot of these bastards. He'd appeal if he were found not guilty."
Counselor: "We really should do something about the randomness of these strip searches."

(There was universal agreement on this point as well.)

Parole Officer: "I would really like a comprehensive definition of normal procedures."
Man in Charge: "Normal procedure is that residents carry out all orders."
Man in Room: "Did his case counselor say, 'At no time did my client refuse to submit to the strip search?' "
Another Man in Room: "I don't know. We don't have to get it all down in writing."

(Inmate N. was found guilty and given the punishment of being able to see only clergy and lawyers for 10 days.)

Others, of course, refuse to enter into such displays about themselves; but in refusing to perform in the ritual, they are nevertheless cooperating in its function. In a letter to his father, George Jackson depicts the attitude of many inmates to whom we spoke in deciding to adopt such a posture of non-cooperation:

> Although I would very much like to get out of here [Soledad Correctional Training Facility in California] in order to develop a few ideas that have occurred to me—although I would not like to leave my bones here on the hill if it is a choice between that and surrendering the things that make me a man, the things that allow me to hold my head erect and unbowed, then the hill can have my bones
> . . . . I may not live another five minutes, but it will be five minutes definitely on my own terms. [Jackson, 1970, pp. 101–102]

Nevertheless, even non-cooperation in the ritualized hearings results in the affirmation that the convict was all along the kind of person who deserved his treatment—a treatment, in fact, that would best 'cure' his malaise.

Ordinarily, when a defendant, under conditions which fairly offered
an opportunity to reply, stands mute in the face of an accusation,
the circumstances of his silence may be taken against him as evidence
indicates an admission of guilty. [Mulbar, 1951, p. 62][f]

Disciplinary hearings in Vermont's maximum security prison are elaborately
structured to provide "legal safeguards" whereby the proceedings take on the
semblance of due process. Far from such safeguards changing the basic symbolic
effect of the procedures, they increase the potency of the hearings as a display
of the character of the inmate. In the face of all the protection afforded him,
they imply, he still looks to be the kind of person we have claimed him to be.
Further, and equally devastating, using the "safeguards" almost always turns
into a comic and desperate performance on the part of the inmate.

Inmate after inmate at the Vermont State Prison called witnesses, themselves convicted felons, to "testify" and testified on their own behalf only to
be met on the part of the board with glaring disbelief. The fact, of course, is
that the "witnesses" already had a relationship to the board independent of
the role of mere witnesses as usually obtains in a courtroom proceeding.[g] Such
a relationship either must be systematically denied by the board—a difficult
if not impossible task since several of them had daily contact with the witnesses
as their custodians, a relationship which is precarious enough—or obliges board
members to deny the saliency of the terms of that relationship for that brief
moment in the hearings. Justice Frankfurter's statement concerning due process depicts it as requiring "an evaluation based on a *disinterested* [our emphasis]
inquiry." What we are arguing is that the very notion of what an inmate is and
the social structure of the staff–inmate relationship precludes "disinterest" in
any real sense. (Cf. Rochin vs. California 342 U.S. 165 (1952) for a fuller statement on due process.)

In short, despite legal safeguards, the board must be concerned about the
implications of their playing a game that calls for impartiality. For the success
of such a stance permits the possibility that the witnesses are in some respects
creditable. Even the momentary credibility of an inmate in the formalized

---

[f]Quoted in Goffman [1969, p. 125].

[g]The double bind here is obvious. Even when the board consists of "outsiders" these
outsiders still stand in a social relationship to the inmate. When that relationship is denied
by the "outsider," on occasion he or she is quickly dispatched by the administration. For
example, we made a practice, when meeting inmates, of shaking their hands and calling them
Mister rather than by their first name. Both guards and administrators were obviously
shocked by this practice and claimed that there was something wrong with *us*. Usually when
outsiders do serve on disciplinary boards, their outside status is questionable even in organizational terms. For example, when a judge ordered such a restructuring of the disciplinary
board at the New Hampshire State Prison, one of the "outsiders" was a trustee of the prison
and a member of the political party of the governor. The whole notion of who stands as an
outsider to the prison is fully discussed in Chapter 7.

ceremonies of the prison is totally incompatible with the institution's need to claim that the marked difference between inmate and keeper speaks to something about the character of each rather than the political arrangements of which such differences are an expression. For without the assumption of this *inherent* difference, the logic of the institution is open to question.

As Goffman [1969, p. 40] has pointed out, there are many social settings where the "observer is likely to try to conceal from the subject the strategic fact that assessment is occurring." In the prison, however, the custodians even in their capacities as "impartial" members of a disciplinary board are concerned to do just the opposite—that is, they must under all occasions display not mere assessment but assessment of *precisely the characteristic*, if not behavior, that the inmate is trying to disprove.

The dilemma is apparent. Inmates are called up on what appear to the neutral observer as petty deviations from petty regulations on the grounds that these regulations are necessary for the smooth running of the institution. Nevertheless, during the hearings, members of the hearing board must attest to the essential difference between themselves and their charges, "a difference between two constructed categories of persons—a difference in social quality and moral character" [Goffman, 1961, p. 111], without which the rationale for the institution loses its force. Only by a finding of guilty can the contradiction be resolved, and the ceremonial function of the hearings maintained. When inmates complain that such hearings are "monkey-courts," they are not talking about the failure of legal safeguards but the ceremonial functions of the proceedings no matter how primped in legal refinement.

The role prescribed for an individual in an institution not only specifies certain patterns of behavior but also serves as an implicit definition of what sort of person he is. We have argued that behind the penitentiary lies the doctrine that individuals incarcerated are "suffering" from a willful inability to be rule-following members of the body politic. The abundance of rules, disciplinary boards, hearings, elaborate hierarchies of infractions, and penalties are not only institutional resources for presenting evidence that makes this a plausible picture of the inmate, they also explain and justify to other inmates the central feature of prisons—repression.

> Most inmates will admit and even require the keepers to assume this function. They understand that the metal detector which uncovers a file intended for an escape attempt will detect a knife intended for the unsuspected back of a friend. Much as they complain of the disciplinary court which punishes them for their infractions, they are grateful for the swift and stern justice meted out to inmates who loot their cells. [Sykes, 1958, p. 36]

This quotation is from a well-known book on prisons and is cited approvingly by the President's Commission on Law Enforcement and Administration of Justice [1967, pp. 178-179]. Yet, the atmosphere of most disciplinary hearings differs markedly from what such a description would lead one to believe. Far from dealing with matters that are of concern to inmates, such hearings direct their attention to infractions of rules that inmates find both random and capricious.

In the New Hampshire State Prison the most frequently heard complaints from inmates *about other inmates* had to do with aggressive homosexual attacks. Because this problem in prisons has received such widespread attention,[h] it will be sufficient only to point out that in almost 2 years of observation at several such institutions we did not see one disciplinary charge brought against the *aggressive* homosexual partner. When there is a "crack-down" on homosexual behavior, it is invariably against those "who are conventionally obvious—that is, those who are excessively effeminate" [Gagnon and Simon, 1972, p. 228]. This position is reflected in the administration of rules concerning homosexual behavior that effectively excludes those for whom most inmates have the most *fear*.

More complaints were heard about the random enforcement of rules than of rule infractions on the part of other inmates. When behavior is admonished, it tends to fall under the general heading of insubordination. Yet insubordination is not the exclusive property of inmates. Several studies have focused on custodial insubordination in the face of changing prison policy. But when such insubordination on the part of guards *does* surface, administrators usually see it as rationally linked to the dangerous circumstances in which the guard must work (see Chapter 4). It is interesting to note how guards trade on what administrators have often claimed is true of prisons—that the place is dangerous!— when they ask for increased appropriations. When administrators *question* insubordination, and thus by implication the dangerous quality of the work, their days are numbered. Ex-Commissioner Boone of Massachusetts is just one recent case in point.

Recently, the guards at the Florida maximum security facility who refused to open the cell doors to let the inmates out to work were refusing to obey orders of the warden in the process. The dispute was not resolved until the Commissioner of Corrections interceded. To the date of this writing, not one guard has been brought up on charges of insubordination. In discussing the matter, staff members of the institution strongly suggested that it was totally

---

[h]See, for example, Lindner [1948, 201-205]. The reader is counseled, however, to read such reports with a jaundiced eye since both scientist and guard share a predisposition to see aggressive sex on the part of inmates as an understandable response to a sexually depriving environment, but *submissive* sexual response—the queen—is seen as deviant. Of course, this mirrors what the society itself holds out to be normal male sexuality. Rape in prisons gets just about the same response it gets on the outside—"what was done to provocate it?"

understandable that the guards acted in self-defense even though this involved the very behavior these same officials will not tolerate from inmates, who might equally claim that they are under threat.

The cogency of the inmates' fear at the same institution is graphically displayed in a set of depositions taken in connection with a riot at that prison:

> *Investigator from the State's Attorney's Office*: "Are there any others that you can identify that assaulted any of the officers or other inmates out there?"
> *Custodian*: "There's a lot of names that I know that's out there but I don't know, it's hard to put a nigger's face with a nigger name."
> *Garment Factory Vocational Officer*: "I know they [the black inmates] wanted to kill us. That's their nature."

Swearing, failure or refusal to work and showing disrespect to guards are the major infractions dealt with by the disciplinary committees. When institutionally threatening events *do* take place, disciplinary hearings are the *last* of the proceedings.[i] After a general strike in New Hampshire, strikers were kept in their cells for various lengths of time. It was only after the administration was prepared to remove the individual strikers from their cells and send them back to work that they were called up individually before the disciplinary board. The hearing room took on the semblance of a principal's office:

> *Hearing Man*: 'Do you plan on making any more trouble?"
> *Inmate*: "No sir."
> *Hearing Man*: "Do you want to go back to work?"
> *Inmate*: "Yes sir."
> *Hearing Man*: "Were you part of them that started that whole business?"
> *Inmate*: "No sir."
> *Hearing Man*: "All right, you can go back to work but keep your nose clean and stay away from [another inmate]."

The Moral Community

Not only is force alone an extremely unstable means of controlling population, it is in direct contradiction to the doctrine of a liberal state whose legitimacy claims to rest on the voluntary acquiescence to government.[j] The shift

---

[i]"In Burns v. Swensen (430 f 2d 771, 8th Cir., 1970) the court ruled that a hearing before the statutorily established disciplinary body was not an essential step in confining a man to punitive segregation where there existed evidence that he was properly confined there" [*The Emerging Rights of the Confined*, 1972, p. 107].

[j]On the limitations of force see Lenski [1966], Dahl and Lindblom [1953], and Wittfogel [1957, ch. 4].

from force to authority requires the implication that moral right is on the side of those in control. Thus, techniques must be available that publicly display the moral position of those in control. This is what has come to be called institutionalized power whereby, as part of what appears to be the impersonal operation of the social unit in question, highly ritualized and formalized procedures are made available to the powerful who testify to their superior accomplishments and qualities. The extra punitive power awarded to officials of the maximum security prison, no matter how cloaked in legal regala, is understandable more as part of these legitimizing procedures than an effect of the deviant character of their charges.

The inmate and the custodian must be seen as residing in two different moral universes precisely because the political character of the status arrangements within the prison implicitly suggests that certain conditions must obtain in order to justify the treatment of inmates. That these conditions do not (and cannot) obtain within corporate capitalism we have argued in an earlier chapter. Whether consciously or not, the custodians of the prison must cooperate to produce the semblance of a *moral* community rather than that of a *political* one. However, the rhetoric, on occasion, even surpasses those in control. When one psychiatrist suggested that an older man in prison for sodomy was really not a criminal, the warden responded: "You can get your little red book by Stalin [sic] and get out of here."

As long as a moral rhetoric (whether supportive or critical of the prison system) is substituted for a political analysis, the actual condition of prisons, their development and operation is shrouded in standards of "right." Ceremonies, like disciplinary hearings, are part and parcel of the equipment available to depoliticize the nature of the treatment of crime and criminals. And, of course, it is absolutely in the interest of those in power to have that power seen as an expression of "rights" rather than "might."

6 The Myth of Rehabilitation

The psychology of granting wide choice under pressure to take action is the American or indirect way of achieving what is done by direction in foreign countries where choice is not permitted. Here, choice is limited but not denied, and it is fundamental that an individual generally applies himself better to something he has decided to do rather than something he has been told to do.
—1965 Selective Service Memorandum

If you don't clean up your cell for the nice guy, you have to for the bastard.
—Resident, Vermont Community Correctional Center

As new versions of crime were reconceptualized to meet changing social and, above all, political conditions, the notion of the criminal had to undergo a parallel change. The state had to create a criminal to fit the crime. A failure of political obligation would not characterize the new "problem" inmate because, as we have seen, the conditions for asserting the presence of such obligation no longer obtain. Rather, he must be diagnosed through a technique that is common to all prison systems and is espoused by the American Correctional Association—"classification." Once the new inmate is first "received" (one inmate commented that the language of incarceration is getting more and more like that of a ladies' tea party), he goes through an elaborate procedure designed to diagnose his particular problem and plan his "treatment."

Know Your Inmate

Based on the notion that the individual is suffering from some moral disease, the classification committee acts as a moral "sieve" through which the newly arriving inmate passes to his appropriate security station. In the words of the American Correctional Association:

Classification . . . is neither specific training nor general treatment, but rather the process through which the resources of the correctional

---

NOTE: This chapter was written with the assistance of John Kugler.

institution can be applied effectively to the individual case. [*Manual of Correctional Standards*, 1966]

Classification works on several levels within state correctional systems. If the system is large enough the inmate is first sent to a reception and diagnostic center where, after initial "screening" and "testing," he is classified and, on the basis of that classification, sent to one of the state's minimum or maximum security units. Some states, however, which have no alternatives available, send all convicted felons to a single facility where they are then classified for various positions within that facility.

Supporters of the classification system finds its rationals within the positivistic model of crime that suggests that crime has something to do with essential characteristics of the inmate.

> The factors which contribute to the making of delinquents and criminals are many and complex. . . . Because specific "cures" for any of the different kinds of criminality are as yet unknown, no one technique or service can be said to function effectively as curative in and of itself. [*Manual of Correctional Standards*, 1966, p. 351]

Given the obvious fact that crime, like the common cold, is "caused" separating variations of crime on the basis of causative factors makes good sense both for the individual and the custodial organization. The more serious the crime the more serious the custodial problem and the more necessary is accurate classification.

> Some organized procedures are obviously necessary to insure the best possible kind of integrations, coordination, and continuity of diagnosis, individualized program planning, and the general conduct of care and treatment. [Manual. . ., 1966, p. 351]

Admittedly, social scientists have yet to come up with a definitive explanation for crime. In their efforts, however, it becomes clear that modern penologists and prison administrators have assumed that there *is* a Lochness monster and, when asked for proof, cite the existence of the search. But as is also becoming increasingly clear, it was never the monster that inspired the original search but rather the needs of the penal system to rationalize its own activities.

The creation of the "criminal" (whether he be a vagrant, dope addict, or sexual deviant) requires a social enterprise by which others come to believe firmly that such behaviors are *inherently* criminal. Social resources, then, become necessary.[a] To the extent that "science" treats crime as some naturally

---

[a]There are but two elaborate studies that indicate the process that the creation of "crime" actually is: Howard S. Becker [1963] and Joseph Gusfield [1963]. For a study tracing the effect of these symbolic trappings of control agencies on the conception the 'deviant' holds of himself, see David Matza [1964].

arising phenomena, the science *itself* becomes part of the process of "moral entrepreneurship"—that is, a social resource itself acting to obscure the political feature of the creation of crime.

Such social constructions require some processes that make them seem reasonable in the face of either no evidence or evidence to the contrary. (It is interesting to note that certain classes of "crime" are not explained by scientific theorizing; embezzlement by elected officials seems to escape notice as does polluting, wire tapping and corporate price-fixing. Yet these behaviors are more serious—if seriousness is measured in terms of social costs—than all of those committed by inmates in the New Hampshire State Prison at the time of this writing.) It is, therefore, relevant to look at prison procedures as formally conducted instrumentalities that provide those occasions that display the taken-for-granted aspect of crime as a personal disorder.

"Classification" puts the official stamp on the inmate as to precisely what kind of disease he is suffering from. By this elaborate process, the prison can order, arrange, and in general, shuffle inmates in the name of science, yet it is interesting to note that the process ends up with classification that is tied primarily and at times exclusively to "security" considerations. (That the 'seriousness' of crime is *socially* determined is lost, of course, in the process which claims that there is an equation between "seriously disturbed inmates" and the security risk they are to the institution.) And the process does not stop there. Once classified (in most states the classification is severely limited by the "treatment" on hand; an analogy would be to decide that someone suffering from a brain tumor was not so afflicted because the institution did not have a neurosurgeon), the inmate receives both his job and the degree of supervision he will require. However, with any change in his behavior, the inmate can be reclassified. Thus, the classification board first sets up the degree to which the inmate will be a rule-follower within the limits of his disease. Then the disciplinary committee, which is often made up of those same individuals who make up the classification committee, decides whether or not the inmate did follow the rules; next, acting now as a classification committee, they rediagnose the inmate's problems and send him either into another unit of the prison or change his job to a less favorable one.

The two processes—disciplinary and classification proceedings—work together to produce the reality with which the prison must contend. By claiming that the criminal is a victim of unique circumstances, either personal or environmental, the prison can concentrate on the defects of the criminal.

Up From Punishment

Classification, like the disciplinary rituals, are intended to display the essential character and "problem" of the inmate as being one constitutionally incapable to one degree or another of following authority. Both however, have given way recently to a more dramatic display of the inmates' "sickness." Rather than merely devoting a few hours a week to these celebrations of inherent weakness, whole prisons are now being set aside for this purpose. Patuxent in Maryland and Vacaville in California are the best known examples. The federal system is characterized by several including one in Springfield, Missouri. It is difficult to know just how many such facilities are currently being organized along this modality, but the recommendation of Dr. William Curran's Harvard-based research team to construct a similar facility on a tri-state basis in New England is probably typical.

The following is a description of the "new" criminal who requires these specialized facilities:

> ... he ... does much to disrupt normal operation of any institution ... he does not respond to disciplinary or external controls. ... [He is] always projecting adversity onto others. ... He is usually verbal ... the only homogeneous factor is that they all cannot adjust satisfactorily in the population of a *regular penal institution*.[b] [*New England Prisoner's Association News*, Jan. 1974; italics added]

For those afflicted with what may someday be called "penal syndrome," new authority regimes are being devised that, under the rubric of rehabilitation, will induce conformity. These new institutions will be staffed with "treatment" personnel who

> cannot be easily manipulated ... has a strong allegiance to established rules and regulations ... [and remains] steadfast on decisions.[c] [*New England Prisoner's ...*, Jan. 1974]

The central element in justifying the forcible incarceration of so many under repressive conditions is the claim that these inmates are otherwise incapable of achieving a law-abiding existence in an equitable society. From this point of view, the prison is "embedded" in a "matrix of the democratic community," and prison administrators are characterized as "adhering to democratic beliefs and practices." If the authority of these figures is questioned, therefore, it is not because of "totalitarianism" but because of the "lack of scientifically tested therapeutic devices" [Sykes, 1956, Vol. 34, No. 3, pp. 257–262].

As we discussed in an earlier chapter, the nature of authority and transgressions against that authority fluctuate with changing political and economic conditions. Further, the degree of harm caused by a particular crime is not easily calculable since, as studies have almost invariably shown, the definition

---

[b]From a report by two staff psychiatrists at the Federal Rehabilitation Institution, Springfield, Missouri.

[c]Ibid.

of crime and its prosecution depend upon constraints exterior to the crime itself. These include the needs of the organization collecting the statistics [Sudnow, 1965] and organizing the work of crime detection [Rubenstein, 1973]; the social class of the offender [Bayley and Mendelsohn, 1968]; and the particular cultural acceptance or rejection of particular kinds of behavior [Gusfield, 1963].)

Obviously, then, neither authority nor deviance is an invariant but is an expression of an already accomplished political, economic, and social situation within which the crime takes place, is adjudicated, and punished. Occurrence, adjudication, and punishment are all equally tied to these constraints. Nevertheless, in the face of this evidence, both prison officials and penologists have displayed a remarkable tenacity in insisting that criminal behavior in general and inmate behavior in particular are manifestations of a faulty social, family, or personal background. This tenacity is matched only by the state's insistence that these "problems" of the inmate are independent of its own form and content. The organized power of the national government may be effective in many areas, but those that "spawn" crime are outside and independent of its activities.

Rehabilitation within prison, then, is just as susceptible to fluctuating conditions as are the inmates to which it is applied. Although identical "treatments" may be employed (e.g., electric shock), it is not clear that it is either punishment or rehabilitation, and therefore, we must consult the competing, contradictory rationales for prescribing it. In sum, offenders have historically been in a position where they might ask the unspoken questions: "What did I do?" and "To whom?" (i.e., where is the locus of jurisdiction for that kind of behavior?). Today, a final question enters: "Who did it?" Is it someone to punish or someone to cure?

> . . . drug therapy holds promise of important contributions to the
> effective treatment of "special offenders." It is our conclusion
> that the use of drugs to control disruptive behavior and to enable
> inmates to take advantage of other rehabilitative programs can be
> much more humane than administrative segregation or more severe
> confinement. [Curran 1973, p. 18] [d]

This prescription for disturbed criminals is tied to social and economic conditions but in a necessarily obscurist fashion. It goes on to recommend that such drug therapy is the treatment of choice since

> . . . other educational and behavior modification programs may
> require intelligence, educational, cultural, and even physical charac-
> teristics of a more selective nature. [Curran, 1973, p. 18]

---

[d]This study was funded by L.E.A.A. in the amount of $188,472.

One Mexican–American inmate who obviously did not have these selective "advantages" reports his reaction to such drug therapy in California's Vacaville:

> I was supposedly misbehaving. At first I was put on prolixim in
> pill form. I had to take it three times a day. The effect was I'd
> suffer muscle spasms that felt like cramps, and I seemed to have
> lost a lot of my coordination, as my arms would now swing when
> I walked. [NEPA *News*, January 1974]

The question is: Is inmate Sanchez's treatment punishment or rehabilitation? The primary prerequisites for deeming someone a candidate for rehabilitative efforts are that (1) the character flaw in question is not really the individual's fault since he acts out of compulsion—without free will; and (2) the benefit from the "treatment" will accrue to the individual not necessarily the society except as an interested but distant spectator, and (3) successful "treatment" implies that the individual will be free to choose desired behavior—that is, the social conditions that allow for such behavior are *a priori* present, and a post-rehabilitative failure to choose proper behavior speaks to the decision of the candidate for rehabilitation and not to the conditions within which he acts. The real attraction for penal officials in labeling their actions as "rehabilitative treatment" is simply that it is "condition-free," i.e., as with the treatment of disease, the individual's actions and reactions are *defined* as being independent of the social order.

Punishment, on the other hand, has three corresponding and contradictory implications. (1) The offender is blamed. Compulsive or environmental factors are deemed to be insignificant, and the offender is presumed to be as free from compulsion as the judge who passes sentence [Hart, 1968]. (2) Punitive efforts derive their justification, form, and content from community rather than individual standards and needs. It may be relevant to consult community values regarding the length of sentence for habitual criminals if one's only interest lies in punishing them. But if one makes a declaration of rehabilitation for those individuals, it is absurd to poll the citizenry for the most appropriate treatment. (3) Unlike the rehabilitative arrangement that presumes that the candidate would enter into it voluntarily if he had the choice, punishment assumes that if given the chance, the candidate for it would make the wrong choice. Thus, punitive efforts forcibly close off certain options for public rather than individual benefit.

The confusion surrounding the dichotomy between punishment and rehabilitation intensifies when one is led into prison. Candidacy for rehabilitation is not tied directly to an act, but for the supposed inability to perform an act, i.e., the failure of an addict to rid himself of his habit. And that failure brands the individual as a *kind of person*; not a person who has committed a *kind of act*. Yet, the actual sentence can only reflect a decision about the responsible commission of a specific, criminal act. Note, for example, the decision in Robinson vs. California [370 U.S. 660, 1962] prohibiting criminal convictions based upon mere status in the absence of an act. In examining the criminal records of inmates at a New England prison, we did note some instances, though extremely rarely, of an inmate's demarcation as "being an habitual criminal," but these were accompanied by specific felony charges in each case.

The striking fact about prison efforts at rehabilitation, then, is that they are by definition extra-legal. *Prison officials must transcend the ostensive reasons for incarceration prior to judging inmates fit for rehabilitative candidacy.* What has been the logical progression to this point? (1) The offender involuntarily arrives at the prison adjudicated as capable of making decisions (as responsible) and guilty of a kind of behavior rather than of being a kind of person. (2) He arrives at an institution with at least a nominal commitment to rehabilitation, which therefore defines the inmate as (a) incapable of choosing otherwise and therefore (b) being a *kind* of person. If given to reflection, he may well realize that (3) *his status as a candidate for rehabilitation was never relevant until he was found guilty for an act by procedures that inherently ruled out rehabilitative candidacy.*

Of course, this does not mean that the inmate is miraculously transformed into a creature who meets any of the requisites for being rehabilitated rather than punished. He is, for example, held responsible for following the prison rule book, which implies an egalitarian approach to disciplinary action and assumes full responsibility on the part of offenders. Yet candidacy for rehabilitation implies individualization of treatment and lack of responsibility for specific acts. There is yet another curious aspect of the dilemma.

All behaviors that therapists see as treatable through rehabilitative measures are also behaviors forbidden by rules and enforced by guards through punitive measures. (Of course one way out of this bind is to simply call these punitive measures rehabilitative measures.) Thus, we frequently found instances where inmates attending drug or alcohol rehabilitation programs were confined to their cells or otherwise punished for using drugs or alcohol. As one inmate, caught sniffing glue in his cell, put it:

> Sure, I knew if I got caught I'd get locked up, but I'm hung up on drugs and it isn't doing me a damn bit of good locking me up. Why don't they do something with their program instead?

Individualization versus Bureaucratic Rule

Rewards in prison are simultaneously grounded in the bureaucratic and individualized models. Inmates demonstrate a reliance on the former when they complain, for example, about work-release programs.

There is absolutely no telling how they choose people to go out.
They have convicted murderers out there who have been here for
twenty years and then guys who got here six months ago. They
have guys with ten years to do and guys with four months to do.

And yet, when an inmate switches to the individualized model and attempts
to display to the classification committee the particular characteristics that he
feels qualify him for work release, he is often met with a denial based on "the
rules" or "our policy." The "against the rules" motto pervades the prison; it
is used for everything from requests for medicine to parole. Yet some individuals *do* get medicine and some do get paroled while others are left struggling
to discover the rule—a rule within either model—that brings benefits when one
believes one has met all relevant criteria.

Individualized treatment, then, has the clear potential to become the
alternative prison legitimization of what would be considered mistakes in a
traditional, rule-governed reward system. It can leave the prison free of criticism—mistakeproof. It does, however, leave correctional officers, formally
called guards and still called "screws" by inmates, in quite a bind. If they
enforce the rules strictly, they are accused of being iron-headed, unprogressive,
and insensitive to individual needs. Of course, the opposite possibility has
"undesirable" consequences. As one inmate said of a certain high-ranking
guard: "He's not doing his job properly because he's doing his job."

The appearance of a diffusion in power that we discussed in a previous
chapter is thus complemented by a split in the conceptual approach to inmates.
The inmate is not only kept guessing who is in charge, he is also kept in the
dark about just "who" he is! This gives the prison a lever to deflect inmate
group action, as complaints of injustice can be swept aside by a claim of individuation for individual treatment, only indirectly tied to social values, cannot
strictly speaking be considered just or unjust. This is a very real reward for
the penal system since it opens the door to all sorts of "value-free" treatment
for which traditional ethical protests are ineffective. Finally, the selective
reinforcement involved in the individualized treatment helps prevent prisoners
from defining themselves as a group, and no one knows if he might be the next
"individual" to receive rewards.

The old inmate standby, "They can control our bodies but not our minds,"
is a constant reminder not to lose what remains of their personal identities. The
drive we noted in a previous chapter to "remain, upon gaining liberty, essentially
the same person I was when incarcerated" is given force by the punitive/thera-
peutic dichotomy. Unlike non-incarcerated individuals who have tactics to
reduce ambiguity in their lives, the inmate is unable to avoid such strains
except by a flat denial of the saliency of one or the other of his treatment
rationales. Emergence of an inmate type depends on which rationale is denied.
To rule out the rehabilitative model is to appear institutionalized. In its extreme

form, it leads to the inmate grumbling about the "country club" atmosphere of
the prison. To rule out the strictly punitive model is to appear rebellious. This
is becoming the norm, as prisoners increasingly accept and then demand that
correctional institutions *correct*. Many of the prisoners at the New Hampshire
State Prison are in on drug charges. While not denying the fact of their usage,
they deny its criminality. For them, the additional rationale of personal
rehabilitation—to the extent that they feel it is required in the first place—is
necessary. And it is given.

But once prison personnel allow that such treatment should take place,
lack of appropriate structure can become material for ambiguity on the part
of the staff and accusation or rebellion by the prisoner. In our interviews with
inmates considered particularly deviant by their wardens, 75 percent spontaneously offered the complaint about their inability to affect their own fate.
Among the "non-deviant" random sample, fewer than half so complained. It
is a fine irony that the very legitimizing rationale—open choice rehabilitation—
employed by the state to control the former group is so often invoked by that
group when they argue against the conditions of their confinement.

The television program *Ironsides* had an episode that underlined a current
dilemma of the modern treatment of criminals. At the beginning, one of Iron-
side's men was dragging an inmate from one state prison to another. He is
ambushed, loses the prisoner, and finds himself being arrested as a vagrant. He
decides to keep his police identity hidden to see what it is like to be arrested.
His experiences are far more gruesome than those we experienced second-hand,
but in a revealing way, that is what one might expect from the media's view of
prisons—twenty men in a nine-by-twelve cell with its implicit, but safe, equation
of penal failure with construction-begging overcrowding. He is deeply affected,
reveals his identity, and resumes his job by taking another inmate back to his
home state's prison. But, experiencing consciousness levels previously considered
unattainable, he benignly tells the prisoner, "Look, if you stay cool, I'll stay
cool. No hassles and we'll have a nice trip." The convict, who looks to be as
innocuous as Murray (the cop) on *The Odd Couple*, shyly nods his head and
mumbles acquiesence. And gently they go.

Of course, one need only anticipate the first unruly prisoner in need of
interstate transmission to see the artificiality of this détente. And, of course,
it is only a television program. But, in fact, a similar situation has developed
at the New England prisons: The administration attempts to balance the "nice
guy and the bad guy" approach throughout all routine contact with inmates.
Just paying lip service to rehabilitation implies at least that much. The absurdity
as well as the true focus of that "balance" is brought home in the following
quotation taken from the files of an inmate. It was made by his case counselor,
a man of the cloth:

> N. needs respect and perhaps we shouldn't make him so comfor-
> table in his cell.

Inmates sense this fragile balance, and it puts them even more on edge than it does their keepers. The label of "treatment" masks the inability of American prisons to fully commit themselves to either simple, unaffected punishment or genuine rehabilitation—whatever that could mean in the context of the social meaning of incarceration—and is nothing short of a mandate for anarchy regardless of staff intentions, which are mixed in any case.

The invidious "nice guyism" permeating the prison not only fails to provide rehabilitative possibilities, it compounds the problems endured by inmates and makes it reasonable to wonder why such actions as the Attica uprising failed to materialize decades ago. In any case, they have materialized today, and it is largely to the problems thereby generated that the following section is addressed.

Escaping the Contradictions: Therapeutic Punishment

It is encouraging to note that we seem to be turning toward a wider use of the indeterminate sentence principle. The number of defendants committed under this plan nearly doubled in the twelve-month period ending June 31 ... immaturity, blind rebellion against some real or fancied social injustice and mental illness [are often] the basic causes of criminality.
                                                —Robert Kennedy, Attorney General, 1961

In light of our discussion of the inherent instability involved in simultaneously applying punitive and rehabilitative criteria to the same inmate and in light of the need for perpetual underemployment, one has good grounds for pessimism concerning vocational rehabilitation programs. Yet, such programs lie at the heart of the justifying apparatus of the American penitentiary. And such programs, or at least the hope held out for major improvements therein, are one of the last available methods for pacifying an agitated inmate population. Reversion to sheer force is a possibility that those in power have repeatedly shown they are willing to use, but it is an obviously unsettling, *revealing* method. Thus, a dangerous tide has been established that must either be swum or dammed. The penal dam that has been sought must be designed to preserve the historic *status quo* while emitting the pacifying aroma of technological progress and individuation. It has been found.

When the civil rights drive evolved into a social movement whose economic demands, concerning not just black employment but *full* employment, exceeded the economy's absorption (cooptation) capacity, a retrenchment process began that went beyond re-arming the police. We have discussed the use of drugging in schools and the ideology of poverty as an inherited black gene. What was needed, in addition, was some sort of theoretical blanket; a statement of movement and stagnation to appease militant and conservative, and to preserve things roughly as they had always been—hence, Benign-Neglect, Black-Capitalism, and so forth. Such disjunctive conjunctions are the hallmark of a society in anguished transition.[e] The anguish and political volubility of recent prison upheavals has led to a synthesis expressed by its own disjunctive conjunction—therapeutic punishment.

Therapeutic punishment is identical to traditional punishment in all respects save one: The issue of *responsibility* for the offender's act is said to be missing. The audience of real benefit is the public; the process trades directly in measurable results, and there need be no pretense of voluntary agreement to enter the program. The social justification is given simply: Nelson, if he were in his right mind, would desire to change his anti-social behavior. Since he is incapable of acting rationally and since his behavior is dangerous, the state is justified in substituting its volition for his and modifying his behavior without his consent.

As a method of legitimization this notion can be incorporated while leaving the prison structure virtually untouched. The conflict over the audience of benefit that ruptured previous efforts is neatly resolved; this approach speaks directly to the sort of results those in charge of penal and political institutions really desire—peace and quiet. Further, it insures that any inconsistencies in the égalitarian underpinning of custodial punishment can be covered by an alternative justification, which, incidentally, manages to skirt the "sensitive" issues of due process and prisoner's rights. As prisons become more professional and technological in orientation, they also become increasingly immune to mistakes for which other institutions would be expected to be accountable. So, "bad" men become "sick" children. And no one, in his right mind, would argue with the notion of total control in that context.

It is potentially the ultimate *Catch-22* for inmates, for it is designed to cut off opposition from both inside and outside. It functions analogously to a politician's claim to be supported by the "Silent Majority." For any critic is no longer silent; and if no longer silent, no longer in the majority. "Silent" acts as the club; "majority" as the term of approbation. Similarly, "punishment" acts as a club and "therapy" as the term of approbation. If a critic claims that the inmate is being "treated" against his will, one responds that he is being punished for an evil deed. If the critic argues that the inmate is not really an evil person, one "agrees" that he is, in fact, a victim of society acting on motives he cannot handle and therefore needs to be treated for his own good.

Part of the difficulty in seeing the potential for total control by the state is provided by a failure on the part of social critics to comprehend fully its implications. Freidson, for example, has stated that:

Increasing emphasis on the label of illness . . . has been at the expense

---

[e]Similar dilemmas have led to such phrases as Protective-Reaction, Deliberate-Speed Peace-Forces, Qualified-Martial Law, Peace-Offensive, and many, many more.

of the labels of both crime and sin, and has been narrowing if not
weakening the jurisdiction of the traditional control institutions
of religion and law. [Freidson, 1970, p. 110]

But our observations would suggest that within the prison structure, the
urge toward such treatment serves to strengthen rather than weaken the foundation, by providing an organized rationale for treating the imprisoned in extra-
legal terms. Instead of replacing one justification with another, the tendency
has been to *combine* justifications. The result is the enlargement of the scope
of inmate behavior coming under the legitimate purview of prison staff.

Another author discusses the problem of converting sheer power into
legitimate authority:

In prison, power must be based on something other than internalized
morality, and the custodians find themselves confronting men who
must be forced, bribed or cajoled into compliance. [Sykes, 1958,
p. 42]

This account, cynical and knowing as it first appears, does not allow us
to fully comprehend the fundamental change the penal system is undergoing.
For the purpose of the new approach is to effect precisely that internalization
of morality the author above dismisses; hence the critical assumption that
inmates must be *socialized* from the ground up, as if from birth.

Are you, the public, going to answer to a small group of inmates who
say, "fire this one, fire that one, let us choose who should be in charge
of corrections," or are you going to see through all the smoke and
suddenly realize that the people sentenced to a correctional facility
were sent there because they could not organize their own life and
conduct themselves in an acceptable manner and should be allowed
to choose who is in charge of a correctional facility? [Unsigned
letter from Vermont State Prison guards, *Valley News*, January 23,
1973]

And so the final link in the choking chain is fitted. Unlike purely punitive approaches that require only *some* form of external justification, i.e.,
public safety (whose effectiveness can be challenged on statistical grounds),
therapeutic punishment is self-legitimizing through its putatively individualized
orientation. It is always "for his own good"—no matter how long it takes.

One of the first institutions devoted to this methodology is Maryland's
Patuxent Institute that is charged with applying psychological concepts to
criminality. The warden and much of the staff are drawn from the "helping"
disciplines and the institution usually acts as its own parole agency.

The process of *entering* Patuxent is interesting and revealing. Take the hypothetical case of Wally Balou who has been apprehended for auto theft. This is, say, the third time he has found himself in this embarrassing position. At the time of the initial hearing, the judge may decide that all is not quite right with Mr. Balou and can therefore order him to Patuxent for "diagnosis and evaluation." If it is found that he exhibits particular pathologies that render him an "habitual offender," then *civil* procedures can be brought against him. The upshot is to order him to the institution until he is sufficiently rehabilitated.

We must assume that in this case, he is placed in Patuxent to prevent him from indulging again in this habit of his, since, in fact, he is not there for any particular *criminal* act. (Remember that it was a civil proceeding that brought him to the institution in the first place.) Now the maximum sentence for stealing a car may be 7 years, but Mr. Balou cannot count on getting out in 7 years. He is not being held for something he did but for something he might likely do in the future. This puts one in mind of an Alice in Wonderland world where the King's Messenger is in prison being punished for a crime that is unlikely to occur until a few weeks from then:

> *"Suppose he never commits the crime?" said Alice.*
> *"That would be all the better, wouldn't it?" the Queen said.*

Five potential Patuxent "patients," challenged the Maryland act that created the institute in the first place. The courts, however, upheld the constitutionality of the institution, holding that "it is within the power of the state to segregate from among its lawbreakers a class or category which is dangerous to the public safety . . ."

> More difficult that the validity of the proposed legislation as against general due process or equal protection attack is the question of whether it can be attacked for vagueness as being a criminal statute which does not sufficiently inform the *accused* [the patient?] of the nature and character of the offense for which he is to be punished. *The principal answer to such attack would seem to be in fact that the statute is not criminal in character.* [Schwitzgebel, 1971, p. 31; italics added]

Ah, back to Alice's world where words are random events. Alice asks our question for us: "The question is . . . whether you can make words mean so many different things." The Maryland Legislature, with the concurrence of the courts, has answered in true Humpty Dumpty form: "The question is . . . which is to be master—that's all."

But the verbal question of who is to be master is paralleled in the concrete question of who is to be master in the broader society. Virtually all of Patuxent's residents are the poor or near poor. Only one-tenth of one percent have a college degree. One doctor, discussing the dearth of professional criminals incarcerated there, says:

> You know, it's just that the professional gunman picks this peculiar
> way of earning a living. A professional gunman, for example, doesn't
> act on impulse or he wouldn't be a professional. Whereas our people
> by and large, one of their characteristics is they're very impulsive.
> [*The New York Times Magazine*, Sept. 17, 1972][f]

Of course the professional killer, and by extension the "professional" embezzler, are deemed responsible for their behavior and thus not fit candidates for a treatment-oriented institution. But what is involved in the "treatment" of the impulsive?

> He spends at least his first thirty—and more often sixty—days on the
> bottom tier, where he is deliberately subjected to the unalloyed
> punishment of solitary lock-up, held virtually incommunicado in
> a nine-by-six-foot cell for almost twenty-four hours a day, denied
> books, letters, visitors, allowed but one shower a week. [Mitford,
> 1973, p. 110]

These are among the variety of modern, space age techniques referred to as "negative-reinforcers," a disjunctive conjunction within a disjunctive conjunction. But positive-reinforcers are at work as well in a four-tiered system of increased responsibility and freedom. As a ranking staff member describes it:

> As he moves upward in the tier system, a patient gains more privi-
> leges.... *It works because that's the way life itself is set up.*
> [*The New York Times Magazine*, Sept. 17, 1972; italics added]

Since the Patuxent population is economically identical to prison populations everywhere else, the average resident knows full well that "that's the way life itself is set up." What they must also know is that the outside system's constrictions may be no different from those inside:

> In nearly 18 years of operation, out of 985 "patients" only 115
> have been released as cured, 332 have been released on mandatory
> recommitment procedures which meet once every third year . . . 38
> percent of all patients are now serving beyond their original sen-
> tences. Of those who were sentenced to terms of five years or
> less, 75 percent are, as they might see it, overdue. [*The New York
> Times Magazine*, Sept. 17, 1972]

---

[f]Extracts from *The New York Times Magazine*, Sept. 17, 1972, are reprinted by permission. © 1972 by The New York Times Company.

Historically, penologists have held that prisons served two audiences: the public and the offender. Thus, as early as the eighteenth century, arguments for solitary confinement were justified in terms of individual rehabilitation.

> Thrown into solitude, he reflects. Placed alone, in view of his crime, he learns to hate it; and if his soul be not yet surfeited with crime, and thus have lost all taste for anything better, it is in solitude, where remorse will come to assail him. [Schwitzgebel, 1971, p. 2]

In reality, however, rehabilitative efforts have always simply been *another way* of generating socially desirable results. We do not treat an offender because he has a problem that *he* desires to end. We treat or isolate him because *we* desire that he change. We would never say of a public hospital that the primary purpose of fixing an injured person was for the public benefit (unless he had a communicable disease, to which crime is often linked.) The public nature of prisons has little to do with their public funding. And newer experiments like Patuxent, which are claimed to be both private in orientation and new in concept, are in reality neither.

> Ultimately the justification of discipline or behavior modification is the safety of the community and not a supposed benefit to the offender. . . . It may be that behavior modification techniques will eventually have a distinct advantage over the more traditional forms of therapy by presenting data clearly demonstrating the effective promotion of public safety. [Schwitzgebel, 1971, p. 4]

Such efforts are new and revolutionary in highly selective ways. They are, after all, grounded in the identical analytic and practical prerequisites as their tired predecessors: (1) they operate in a structure of total power now legitimized through the insanity posited of the inmate; (2) they are allowed to substitute their volition for that of the inmate; and (3) they must trade in directly measurable public results. Above all, what they have done—what they have been *mandated* to do (for prisons do not wag the dog)—is to transcend the enormous contradiction between political doctrine and penal practices.

7 Doctors and Wardens

In former days, when it was proposed to burn atheists, charitable people used to suggest putting them in the madhouse instead; it would be nothing surprising now-a-days were we to see this done, and the doers applauding themselves, because, instead of persecuting for religion, they had adopted so humane and Christian a mode of treating these unfortunates, not without a silent satisfaction at their having thereby obtained their desserts.

—John Stuart Mill, 1859

Psychiatrists are similarly confused. They act as wardens but think they are doctors.

—Thomas S. Szasz, 1963

We have suggested that the prison must maintain moral boundaries between the community and the inmates if incarceration is to be organized in a fashion allowing for the smooth functioning of the prison—even if that smooth functioning requires the assumption that it *can* become unsmooth at any moment. But, as we have argued, the political conditions within which the prison must operate suggest that these boundaries are imposed rather than inherent and that far from being potentially a full member of the society as it is (the complete Protestant who has strayed), the inmate is *systematically* deprived of the resources for so behaving and the *state* (which is now punishing him) is the party responsible for that deprivation. Far from being uniquely "different" from the non-incarcerated population, he is statistically no more guilty of criminal behavior than many who simply escape state notice. Far from the conditions of his deprivation putatively *causing* crime—producing a kind of immorality or pathology in the inmate—it seems to be the case that it is the presence of these conditions that merely allow the state to incarcerate him.

The Insider and the Outsider

Mere physical incarceration of offenders has never been enough since it was the reciprocal of being "free," and freedom, it was claimed, was the expression of being a kind of person. The "liberal" state liberated men from outward constraints by making constraint an inward affair. Insofar as the state removed the right of freedom, it was justified by the claim that without such interference the individual would never be that kind of inwardly constrained person—but forever an outsider.

Those "outsiders" are, then, socially and politically constructed types of persons, and anyone who comes in contact with them is required to display appropriate regard for the psychological boundaries that exclude them from ordinary civil behavior.

Some time ago, a social scientist [Hughes, 1962] wrote a piece called "Good People and Dirty Work," based on reports he collected from German citizens after World War II regarding their state of knowledge concerning the extermination of the Jews. His work is part of a growing collection that suggests that (1) the very conditions about which "good people" would in the abstract complain are in fact being maintained by (2) people who in many respects strongly resemble those to whom the "dirty" work is done—they are pariahs.

With regard to the prison, it is suggested that while the good people may in the abstract complain of inequities and so forth, they allow such practices to continue by not personally involving themselves but rather relegating the chore to the "less desirable" elements of the community. In Hughes' argument, it is assumed that part of the explanation for such social arrangements is that the "good people" can have it both ways: They can take measures against those whom they see as a threat while at the same time deny any responsibility for it.

More recently, a state-sponsored commission [*Attica*, 1972] claimed that prison riots are an effect on the *failure* of this arrangement. In the Attica Report it was argued that black inmates rioted precisely because their keepers were more like the "good" people than they were. The guards were rural and white, the guarded were urban and black. This argument, then, presupposes that there is some *social benefit* to be obtained by having the dirty work done by dirty people. The dirty element will be handled better by people similarly attired.

This convoluted use of Hughes' ideas aside, we find his work a valuable insight into the management of ideologically spawned deviance. And, in general, it is descriptive of the prison. *But sometimes it is helpful to have the dirty work done by even "better people" and thus ratify the social necessity of the work.*

This, then, is the story of "good people" doing their share of the dirty work.

On Being "Good People"

What we have suggested is that the distinction between crime and punishment is exclusively a political distinction—that is, what is done by the state as a punishment *minus* the legitimacy of the state would look like a crime. And the legitimacy of the state is always a political affair. The upshot of Hughes' argument is that there is something dirty about "legalized" crime and that our society is happy to have the pariahs either behind bars or directly in front of them; but most certainly out of sight.

The hangman with his identity-hiding hood is gone; the firing squad with but one active bullet among dozens of blanks is no longer a feature of penal life; the "contractor" who took on prison laborers is no longer the social outcast. No, the modern manager of incarceration is ideally a Ph.D. or M.D., a university-based professor, and upstanding member of his church where he gives occasional lectures on the problems of the prison. He has become a public person.

And the sheer stature of this public person will maintain the boundary and integrity of the prison. Where such resources are not directly available to the prison, there are always outside agencies that will import the experts. One New England prison's psychiatric services were almost completely funded by L.E.A.A. So armed with this generous granting, we set off to the maximum security prison to begin our understanding of the deviant offender, the inmate who was failing to adjust to his incarceration.

Our first dilemma was, of all things, how to dress! The warden insisted that the usual attire of the researchers—standard blue jeans and work shirts—simply would not do. We looked too much like the inmates who, as part of their prison garb, wore exactly the same thing. We were stunned. We had not really given much thought to the distinction between ourselves and the prisoners. It was easy enough to sense but harder to understand the heavily packed social arrangements that provided the visibility of that distinction. We were told that it was merely for security. A guard could spot a pair of blue jeans and know he was looking at an inmate, but if we—the outsiders—were to dress identically we might be mistaken for an errant prisoner. We bought the argument and only months later noticed that inmates with trustee status—wearing those same blue jeans—came and went within the prison without problem. Obviously the guard in the control tower looked for more than blue-clad legs to determine whether the person attached to them was legitimately out on his own. Like much of what was to follow, the argument we were given broke down, leaving in its wake a residue of the feeling of simply having been had.

So, finally, there sat some very well-dressed men and women awaiting their first inmate. Our clothing attested to the fact that we were most certainly different from them—maybe in respects deeper than mere attire but *at least* in that respect. But before we got to the inmate we had to get through the doors.

The architecture of the prisons we visited was strikingly similar not only with respect to their various claims on antiquity and bleakness but in terms of the remarkable contrast between that condition and the rather modern control rooms they all had.

Enclosed by bullet-proof glass, sparkling with elaborate electronic equipment; with a push of a button, doors blocks away opened, closed, locked. Behind the bullet-proof glass stood the prison's Wizard of Oz! The warden might have had the last say, but our man in the booth held the last button and we were damned if we knew how to get his attention. We would stand at the mirror to which he looked (or so we hoped) at the bottom of the stairs; we would feel that he was ignoring us; four times we heard that buzzer opening up other doors; why wouldn't he open ours? We smiled at the mirror; the mirrored smile looked back at us and the door still didn't open. We were embarrassed. We looked like the right kind of persons to be admitted; we had cut our too-long hair, shaved the beards, put on the flannel trousers, and the women wore skirts, and the door still didn't open. Happy was the day that we could tuck ourselves in with a returning group of inmates or the warden and his party lately from lunch and stand waiting for the door to be opened.

We were outsiders and we knew it, but how did *they* know it? The door was the first of the reinforcements to our belief that somehow things we had expected to be true about ourselves were *socially* arranged and could be taken away at a push of a button. If the Wizard of Oz could give the tin man his heart, he could, in all probability, take it away. We who had passed through doors, real and metaphorical, stood at the bottom of the steps trying to get into prison.

The first step was to realize that those social arrangements upon which the prison relies hardly stop with the inmate—if they did it wouldn't work. We were shown quickly enough that just standing waiting for someone else to decide when you could pass through a door could make you enormously self-conscious. Something of yourself slips away. A world of Wizards of Oz with magic buttons is also a world of cowardly lions and tin men.

But why make *us* the cowardly lions? We were there on a federally funded grant applied for by the prison administration. We were there to help *them* help *others* help themselves. The world in which we lived suggested that we had all the power. We were members of the "good" people and had the right tests tucked under our arms prepared to find out why inmates behave badly. But there was a test tucked under the arms of the prison management as well, and that was whether we would accede to the notion that it was right and proper that there *should be* the Wizard of Oz; that we were legitimately opened to being checked out; and that the *threat* was everywhere. And the longer we *patiently* waited, the greater the evidence grew that this was a very dangerous place indeed and that we *knew* it.

Our first step into the prison was to be testimony that the assumptions upon which the prison based its credibility were at least plausible. The bell rang, we pushed the door open and went in. We started to be insiders.

The Random Inmate

A battery of psychologists, psychiatrists, social workers, nurses, and a few strays began to make their way down to the state prison three or four times a week for over a year, testing, probing, interviewing, dodging. Charged with diagnosing and treating the "disturbed" offenders, we were given a list by the warden of all those inmates who were "sick." But being good scientists, we thought it important to know what a non-disturbed offender looked like. We wanted a comparison group.

The warden had other ideas. We asked his permission to develop a randomly selected group of inmates so as to provide this comparison. He looked at us as though we were mad.

"I know a disturbed inmate when I see one."

"Of course we aren't doubting that for one minute but what we need to know is how this inmate is different from those who are not disturbed."

"Because the disturbed ones give us trouble, that's how they are different."

"Of course, but don't you want to know why?"

Here the warden looked perplexed. He asked how we were to find these non-disturbed inmates. We told him that we would simply use scientific methods to pick a random sample. He wanted to know more. We said, "Well, we number all the inmates from one on up and then we ask the computer to select forty random numbers and then pick those whose numbers correspond to the numbers spewed out by our computer."

We returned with the randomly drawn list of inmates. When we showed the list to the warden he became very excited and congratulated us and our computer.

Running his finger down the list, he virtually picked out the names of every two or three inmates, saying, "Yes, this one is sick." "This one is really a trouble maker." "Yes, you will certainly find this one psychotic."

We were amazed. If random, the list should not have included all those sick people—or maybe everyone was sick? Yet a third possibility: once your name is on a prison list wardens are put in the frame of mind that there must be some purpose behind it all. Would sheer randomness be an untenable thought in a prison? Psychologists have long held that there will be a relationship between the way a person behaves and the way he perceives [Bruner and Goodman, 1947]. Presented with what should have been a fairly neutral stimulant—a random sample—the warden immediately perceived more sickness than chance alone would have suggested.[a] In the absence of any experimental investigation of the *warden's* behavior, we can only guess at its cause.

There was yet a second aspect to picking a random sample that seriously disturbed the administration—one that foreshadowed many of the problems with which we would be faced until the end of our research.

We had come into the prison at their request, or at least at their initiation. Before we would be allowed to hire even a research assistant, we would have to introduce him or her to the warden. Woe betide us should we forget this rule and bring in someone whom the warden didn't know. Control was to be his.

---

[a]Chance obviously played a role in the sanction of deviants in the "ordeals" (see Chapter 1). The replacement of these practices by "modern" methods is predicated on the notion that there are available skills found in professional agencies for determining guilt and its treatment. Chance is obviously a hazard in the game of law enforcement in general [Aubert, 1959].

But we were professionals and running through *that* ideology was a notion that how we did our work was within our own control. In fact, that is what set us apart, distinguished us, gave us our mandate. We knew better than the layman how to do the work. Bringing us into the prison opened up a Pandora's box for the warden since this implied that, at least with regard to what we did, he was not to be the absolute authority.

As we suggested earlier, the authority of the state rests on certain assumptions that inmates have seriously begun to question. Insofar as this is the case, the one chink in the armor of both the "liberal" state and its coercive institutions is the notion of precisely what threatened the warden—the locus of authority. In general, criminology has buttressed the claims of the prison that it is the failure of the *person* when authority is questioned:

> The Greeks' prescription was for . . . a prudent moderation between self-expression and self-control. This ancient prescription is relevant to the study of criminogenesis, for the people who recognize no external authority will have no internal authority. They will have no reliable self-control that limits their actions *vis-a-vis* others. What one wants to do will be what one does. The person who asks, "What's wrong with that?" is already infected. [Nettler, 1974, p. 259]

In prisons, as well as in criminology, the terms of the authority and the ends to which it will be put are not seen as particularly relevant. Hence, the prison in both its operation and rationalization has let loose a doctrine that necessarily leads to a kind of tyranny quite independent of the particular psychology of those individuals with the socially accredited authority to which inmates must respond. Our trouble was simply that *we* had not expected to come in for the same treatment. In a sense, once the prison found a doctrine of punishment that fit what the state was putatively about, it had to develop a kind of morality that included everyone. Authority was the keystone to the prison precisely because it had defined crime as a *personal* failure or inability to respond to authority.

Crime, then, becomes less a kind of behavior and more a kind of human nature. From this there easily evolves a whole metaphysics—a world view. And world views brook no exceptions. Once in the prison as either inmate or professional, this world view becomes the standard against which all behavior is judged.

To be accepted by the prison staff meant to either acquiesce or *affect* acquiescence to this world view on called-for occasions. But the latter was no easy task since noting authority is the kind of behavior that is only noticeable in its absence—that is, it is the kind of behavior that "gives rise to specific negative sanctions if not performed, but which, if it is performed, passes unperceived as an event" [Goffman, 1963, p. 6].

The upshot is that every behavior is potential material for assessment of whether or not due respect for authority is being displayed.

In *asking* to take a random sample, we were attempting to put ourselves in a properly respectful position with regard to "management." What we did not realize is that the very act of performing a task that brought us into daily contact with inmates carried a potential for not displaying regard for authority. We would be acting on our own for our own "scientific" reasons that might have little to do with the reasons of that management.

The matter was settled, or so we thought, to our liking. But, as it turned out, the administration kept the perogative of censoring at will the list of inmates we had scheduled for interviews. This provided us with a dilemma that became something of a joke, for we would have to spend much time seeking out the proper person to grant us authority for the interviews knowing full well that we were doing something that made little sense. When we finally stumbled upon the proper authority of the day (and for such a formalized structure that person seemed a variable that behaved almost randomly), we stood in jeopardy of being treated as we knew we should be treated—"Why are you bothering to get permission for something like this? Aren't you people responsible to do your own thinking?" It became a game for all treatment and research people to try to discover what rules would be in effect on any given day with regard to how one got to see any particular inmate without giving up our "professional autonomy."

Underlying the ascription of crime as a form of mental illness is the notion that any sane person will not question the authority of the state. When authority is made a matter of moral principle and psychological health, any behavior that is an abuse of that authority becomes a symptom of a failure of morality or a sign of illness. Insofar as the experts who were there to diagnose this "illness" failed to respect that authority themselves, there could quickly arise the belief that either they *too* were ill (i.e., criminal) or that being a criminal entailed something quite different from the "illness" that the prison existed to "cure."

> ...the American conception of deviance as illness becomes a way
> to reassert the Puritan tradition that there can be no human behavior
> that is not an active search for secularized salvation and in the service
> of the commonwealth of true believers. [Pitts, 1961, p. 705]

The equation is tricky but one that prison personnel seemed to have totally internalized. Crime is an offense to the state because the state is the embodiment of authority, and this authority, it is claimed, is based on *natural* principles (see Chapter 1). Insofar as one commits a crime, one is acting out of accord with these natural principles, is therefore behaving irrationally, and must be ill. If those who were there to diagnose the illness equally displayed such "irrational" behavior, then either such behavior was *not* irrational or the doctor was in need of some prison "cure" himself.

The Experts from Expertland

Robert Sommer [1963] has described the world of the experts as made up of nomads who really never travel. Academics go and come but always return to the "same" environment replicated in hundreds of universities, medical schools, and other such institutions, each of which look very much like the other. We are citizens of no country; responsible to the truth and the truth alone. This presumes that truth has some unidimensional quality that, if one is just expert enough, will be revealed. This view of the truth is not only paralleled in those institutions dedicated to arriving at it—unidimensional themselves—but also in the very instruments that will best serve its purposes.

The "testing" of inmates, then, was to be done through one of these instruments—a psychological test that was respected in expertland for its high validity and reliability. Now the very idea of such criterion—validity and reliability—asserts that what is true is independent of political conditions within which one gets at, tells, and acts on the truth. Our training had told us that of course wardens and their employees had special interest in convincing us that some of their inmates were "sick," disturbed, and disturbing. With our instrument, though, we could test the inmate directly and avoid this contamination of the truth.

Armed with our test we would act as the true expert, value-free to the end. We marched in and found how wrong we were and, in the process, what the prison was really all about.

But, of course, before we could use our test we had to get to the inmate, and, as we have said, this was no easy matter. Stories from various sources had engendered a fear bordering on terror in our hearts. We had visited one institution that was patrolled by half-starved neurotic dogs who snarled on cue at any passer-by. Each prison within which we were to work had its own special arrangement for convincing us that our work was to be carried out in a very special climate—one that was fraught with danger. And knowing, half-smiling looks we received from the "management" as certain inmates' names were mentioned confirmed the worst.

Our mental state was not enhanced by the discovery that one of the first men we would be interviewing was convicted of, among other things, "assault with intent to disfigure." We reassured ourselves that we were safe, after all there were bullet-proof enclosures and even the National Guard, if necessary. The women on the team were told to stay with one of the men and, for the first time, those men *really* regretted sexism—with whom could *they* stay? But there we were, with our valid and reliable test but wishing for a valid and reliable guard, ready for our first inmate—the disfigurer!

In walked a beaten-down man of slight physique in his mid-thirties. He probably had no reason to be curious about the fact that while most interviews would be done with one interviewer, or at most two, this time there were four of us cramped into a tiny room adjoining what was referred to as the "hospital."

The inmate was seen only after we had gone through his file. We told the interviewers not to treat the file as some true statement concerning the inmate's past, but merely as part of the environment with which he had to deal. An inmate's being charged with many crimes may not tell one much about his criminality but certainly says a great deal about a set of "facts" to which he is expected to have the proper attitude or at least some attitude. Like mental hospitals, prisons through the incantation of the treatment doctrine have a "legitimate claim to deal with the whole person." However, this license hardly could extend to everything the inmate did and, as we shall show, necessarily focuses on what is conceived to be organizationally relevant. The license then is better depicted as one that allows record keepers to define any behavior as having relevancies for the record [Goffman, 1961, pp. 154-160].

Given that files are used to measure the in-house development of inmates, we thought they might be inaccurate with regard to their experiences in the past and subject to "institutional" error with regard to the present but still contain some informational value. We diligently read the files on each inmate and, in bored moments, looked at files of those inmates we would probably not see for a week. We noted the number of rule infractions, the disciplinary hearings, the number of times the inmate failed to report to work, and in general his life history in the institution. When we consulted our notes some time later, we were surprised to see that there was no category for the inmate's "improvement." Searching through the files once more we came upon not one instance of any favorable conduct of the inmate—except for obligatory work reports.

During this period of rechecking, a new research effort was being mounted within the program with which we had been working, and we attended a meeting of the new group to discuss "scientific" methods for measuring the inmate's improvement. We pointed out that the "records" themselves would be of little use since they did not seem to contain any category for displaying approved behavior; there was space only for behavior that the institution negatively sanctioned. The new researchers then inquired about constructing their *own* instrument for such measurements and asked for our observations of possible indications of improvement on the part of individuals in the prison. We were again at a loss to give them help.

Although the prisoners' files displayed no positive information, we were willing to explain this fact by the attitude of the guards and administrators. While we felt that most of the information collected was true, we believed that they purposefully gave a one-sided view of an inmate's day by systematically neglecting his increasing capacity for improvement—willingness to become a law-abiding citizen. But our conversation with the new researchers made clear to us that far from the records being a distortion of prisoners' behavior, *they were totally accurate*. What we began to suspect was that inmates have a limited set of behavioral possibilities in prison—that is, while he may not swear, show up for work late, get into fights, and so forth, these are not noteworthy events in themselves. It would be humanly impossible to note the occasions when inmates obeyed orders, responded positively to their work, and the like, since the fact is most inmates do this all the time. To note systematically what the culture holds out as desirable behavior is to convert into "news" or "events" that which by cultural definition are "non-events."

There is one way of transforming these non-events into something that becomes socially visible and that is to *become* something one had not previously been—that is, to display oneself when entering the institution as the worst of all possible persons and then systematically, at the end of a few months, become *better*. Inmates often remarked to us that this was the one tactic that guaranteed an early release—sure parole.

Researchers have long supported the idea that social approval will play an important role in attitude change. However, some studies have shown that this is a function of the individual's desire to maintain membership in a group. Those to whom the group has high value will be most strongly influenced by the group's attitude toward him and thus be more likely to come into conformity with the group's expectations [Cohen, 1964]. But when this process is truncated by the sheer impossibility of displaying oneself as an adequate member at the start, then the approval of the group takes on a forced importance. In a sense, prison custodians and administrators have a built-in mechanism that inflates their importance to the inmate.

By systematically denuding the institution of those social arrangements whereby certain behaviors can be looked upon and *noted* as displaying some desired quality, the inmate is forced into delaying his acceptable behavior until it appears that the desired activities are a function of behavior of the custodians and an effect of the prison regime. In effect, this was managed success.

But the experts were hard pressed to note this effect of imprisonment for some time, and we continued to pore over the records. For what else had we? We did not stop to consider that it was precisely because we had nothing else that the inmate began taking on some very peculiar characteristics quite apart from anything he might have been. And it goes without saying that most inmates were very much aware of this. Upon entering the interview room, his eyes would almost automatically go to the table where we were in the habit of stacking the records of all those who would be interviewed on that day. Finally it dawned on us that far from the kind of records we kept on *ourselves*—our *vitae* that included only those reports of ourselves which gave us the greatest pride and over which we had much control—the inmate's records contained all that he was most ashamed of and over which he had no control.

We finally stopped reading the records. Was this a scientific judgment or a political act? If the records were scientific, it was political. If the records were political, it was scientific. In either case, the experts had begun to move out of expertland.

The Expert as Imputational Specialist

In order for the prison to work within the new doctrine of rehabilitation
and correction, it must make salient in all its operations the idea that the inmate
is a kind of person. Further, the more the doctrine of punishment departs from
the practices of the state, the more necessary it becomes to rearrange, add to,
and redefine prevalent social conditions within which this new identity will be
used by prison personnel in rationalizing their activities. Far from the man on
the street, however, automatically and correctly imputing certain characteristics
to these socially constructed persons, what is required is an "imputational
specialist"—that is, specialists whose training, interest and well-being are all
aimed at discovering "in the empirical world those sorts of people they have
been trained to see" [Lofland, 1969, p. 136] .

Today, the school, the university, the family, and the prison all have their
resident psychiatrist, or would have if funds were available. This dispersal of
psychiatric personnel increases the sheer reasonableness of imputing to any
institutionally specific problems the character of psychological disorder. The
number of inmates who became "ill" during our prison stay increased more than
100 percent over the number we were told were ill when we first came to the
prison.

But this "becoming" ill should not be seen as developing a set of symptoms
that were once absent but as a reflection of the prison's ability to redefine previous behavior as indicative of pathology—all, of course, with the help of the
"imputational specialist."

Instead of a prisoner being dangerous, he is now a psychopath. Instead of
his having rough friends, he is now a sociopath. Instead of his being just bellig-
erent, he is now delusional. Our language, dress, computer, and Ivy League
base endowed what we did with a kind of seriousness, in fact solemnity, that
the prison alone could not have achieved. Inmates entering our "examination
rooms" took on a look of seriousness that one expects to be offered only to
the most sacred of personages. Objective tests, various pieces of equipment to
diagnose sub-cortical brain damage, and recording events, both in our special
folders and with our video-tape machines, heightened the drama of the event
and the sacred quality of its effects. Lopland could have been describing our
'team' when he said:

> Given the imagery of gravity and expertise which surrounds such
> specialists, it is not surprising that the mere fact of their codings
> can be sufficient for others to grant them credence and that the
> mere fact of their having coded [the inmate] . . . is sufficient to
> pre-sell this coding to a multitude of others. [Lopland, 1969,
> p.156; italics added]

Quite apart from the always open question of how much therapy was actually accomplished, there is no question about the imputational effectiveness of our presence. By simply being on the scene as experts, we became (whether we liked it or not) "imputational specialists" and in doing so created the kind of person the prison said it was treating.

The saliency and use of the expert's official definition of the inmate is, however, like the inmate's own behavior—that is, always controlled by the prison "managers," unless they are one of the managers themselves. Szasz reports the case of Ezra Pound who was found too insane to stand trial by a panel of psychiatrists. When the jury agreed that Pound was of an unsound mind, he was remanded to St. Elizabeth's Hospital where he stayed for 11 years. When the political climate had changed sufficiently, the orginal indictment was dismissed on the grounds that he was too insane to have been tried. In other words, depending on the political context, the psychiatric "evidence" can conclude that a man should be locked up in the security wing of a mental hospital or that he should be allowed to go free.

In charging the jury in the original trial, the judge said:

> . . . you have heard the testimony of all these physicians . . . and, of course, these are men who have given a large part of their professional careers to the study of matters of this sort . . . [Szasz, 1963, p. 203]

But, of course, the judge was wrong. These men had spent a great deal of their lives making judgments that once made were left to others to use, ignore, or twist at their own discretion. How that discretion worked was a matter of politics, not psychiatry.

In a random search through the records of the prison, we found innumerable cases of psychiatric and psychological judgments being rendered that in no way influenced the treatment of the inmate. The solution to the problem, it would seem, would be to turn the power to run the prison over to the "experts" and, of course, this is the movement that typifies the most modern approach to penology. But two important considerations render this judgment inappropriate. The first is that there is absolutely no evidence that criminals are more in need of therapy than any other randomly selected group. The second, and most important, is, as we have stressed, the "treatment" of crime is essentially a political affair, and there is nothing in the training of the experts that would allow them to deal with politics; but there is a great deal that would allow them to *obscure* the political element of corrections.

This obscurantism is the most salient feature of official dealings with the inmate and his problem. For example, the Law Enforcement Assistance Administration, when it does award grants for studying the situation of inmates, always does so within the general model of assuming that his problems are indeed his own. And sometimes so much his own that only his genes are responsible for his behavior. One grant was to develop a study of the chromo-sonal causes of criminality. Another was to study the "mentally abnormal offender" (and to indicate the context-free element of this perspective, it is worthy to note that the study was based in Sweden). Another was more ger-mane to prison conditions, this was a grant to study the alternatives to punish-ment "including techniques of operant conditioning." When the agency does get into the business of the legal structure that *has* incarcerated the inmate, it does so in order "to reduce the number of frivolous and unwarranted prisoner complaints which now clog court calendars." The justification of this grant is that such a reduction will "make prisoners more amenable to treatment by giving them a feeling of being treated fairly. [L.E.A.A. Budget Report, 1971]

Ryan typifies such responses to the problem of the "problem" inmate as the "exceptionalistic" viewpoint

> ... [which holds that problems are] reflected in arrangements that
> are private, voluntary, remedial, special, local, and exclusive. Such
> arrangements imply that problems occur to specially defined cate-
> gories of persons in an unpredictable manner.... They occur as
> a result of individual defect, accident, or unfortunate circumstance
> and must be remedied by means that are particular and, as it were,
> tailored to the individual case. [Ryan, 1971, pp. 16-17]

When we first went into the prison, we were imbued with this "excep-tionalistic" orientation to inmates. When this view did give way to an expres-sion of the prison's responsibility for the condition of the inmate, however, it was still within a framework that did not and could not alter his basic circum-stances.

As the effect of the setting began to wear off, we came to view inmates not so much as dangerous elements who were likely to go for our throats but as sick individuals hiding behind one of any number of psychic defense mechanisms. We noticed, for instance, that a very large number of them were preoccupied with various physical ailments. In almost all cases they had some medical history to back up their claim, but their talk indicated that they had become almost obsessed with whatever problem they had. Our response, of course, was to duly mark this down on the answer sheet to our test, soon to be fed into the computer, and to reaffirm our perception of their mental instability.

In time these "facts" would be used to categorize the inmate population into those who were disturbed and those who were not. The disturbed population presumably would then be treated for their problems. What was necessary to construct this disturbed group, however, was to see their state-ments as a reflection of some underlying problem. Too much attention to the body was scored as a possible symptom. The very act of doing this neces-sitated our total disregard for the conditions within which the inmate lived, conditions so bereft of normal stimuli that one's body might take on undue significance. As this became clearer to us, we began to be aware that the "underlying" problem might be the prison itself. We thought the notion so radical that we treated it as suspect information that we could not let on to prison authorities. But there was a weakness in our humanitarian position, for we were still saying that these inmates were in some respects *different*. We had simply switched the locus of responsibility for that difference from some personal problem to that of the environment. Paradoxically, far from this being a threat to the overall doctrine that kept these men imprisoned, it in fact *supported* the legitimacy of some kind of incarceration.

This movement of our own thought parallels developments on a larger scale in the treatment of the deviant. Originally, evil acts are seen as consequences of problems inherent in the individual himself. This view was essentially that held by the reformists of an earlier age. The more sophisticated version of this philosophy is that the evil encountered in the person is an effect of environmental causes. The evil is still located *within* the individual, only now it is an effect of social or cultural forces. This new idea of ours and other social scientists is not totally unwelcome in prisons, for it allows the locus of attention to remain riveted on the individual offender. Ryan describes the modern treatment personnel in prisons perfectly when he says the following:

> He can, all at the same time, concentrate his charitable interest on the defects of the victim, condemn the vague social and environmental stresses that produced the defect (some time ago) and ignore the continuing effect of victimizing social forces. It is a brilliant ideology for justifying a perverse form of social action designed to change, not society, as one might expect, but rather society's victim. [Ryan, 1971, p. 7]

It might be objected that indeed we were blaming the prison conditions *right then* when we claimed it was the prison environment that sustained the inmates' problems. But minus the authority to do anything about that environment, we simply had no recourse but to continue to treat its victims. Our explanations for their problems were rhetoric, our treatment was control.

State Authority and Psychiatry

The world view of psychiatry and related helping professions has been splittered of late between what is conceptualized as three *competing* ideologies: the somatic—the belief that mental illness is a reflection of organic diseases of the brain; the psychotherapeutic—the belief that mental illness is primarily the result of early childhood experiences; and the sociotherapeutic—the belief that mental illness is caused by social and environmental factors, usually those occurring in the patient's recent life situation [Armor and Klerman, 1968]. But within each ideology is the notion that the patient's problems are essentially his own, how they are worked out is what differentiates each of the competing factions not *where* they are located. This is the reason, of course, why all therapists who have been medically trained will so often resort to drugs and other physical measures; it is the patient who is suffering and it is the patient who will be treated. (This is not to ignore the validity of certain specific individualized cures, but to point up the logical direction and implications of contemporary psychiatry and "social" work.)

While the prison walls contain his body, his body contains his problems. In the absence of our being politically capable of doing anything about his custody, at least some attention could be paid to his "self"—the problem-ridden *person*. Questions we raised concerning the actual daily management of the prisoner were always treated by the prison staff as overstepping the bounds of our mandate. To paraphrase Beckett, we were allowed to crawl eastward on a westward moving ship *and by doing so further propelled it in its course.*

Treating offenders has become almost a catchword in prisons. Our grant was designed to increase therapeutic services to the "disturbed" offender. This, however, was peanuts compared to the money pouring into other facilities for the "treatment of offenders," California has perhaps the epitome of treatment facilities that, while administered by the Department of Corrections, is called "the medical facility," and other jurisdictions have gone so far as to establish "hospitals" where offenders are incarcerated not for law breaking but for being "defective" [Macdonald, 1958, p. 124].

When Vermont began militating for a new correctional facility, for example, it was argued that the old one had become obsolete in terms of the *new treatment modality* [State of Vermont, 1970, p. 22]. In short, the notion that crime is inherently an effect of some mental derangement of the offender has been systematically used by the state to increase its penal budget and thereby its potential for control. Recently, however, the statutes under which this special category of offenders fall have come within the notice of the courts, which have severely questioned the legality of such commitment procedures.

After reviewing these findings, Hickey concludes:

Special statutes under which so-called psychopaths . . . are civilly committed should be repealed as they fail to perform the basic function for which they were enacted—they do not select persons on the basis of dangerousness. They should be repealed because of what they do accomplish—they allow for the indeterminate commitment of persons . . . [Hickey, n.d., p. 15]

The author of these remarks goes on to suggest that rather than these offenders being committed under civil procedure they should instead follow the National Council on Crime and Delinquency in its Model Sentencing Act, which

> . . . provides for the selection, after conviction, of persons on the basis of dangerousness, those persons to be sentenced to terms adequate to protect society from future harm. [Hickey, n.d., p. 15]

In short, psychiatry will move into the prison once the person has been committed for a criminal offense and treat his behavior as though the offense was a mere symptom of some underlying cause. One text on the penal uses of therapy suggests the following:

> The prisoner is confined and treated under an indeterminate sentence, and is released only when his "emotional unbalance" is so relieved as to make it reasonably safe for society to set him free. Thus the length of time that a man stays will be determined not so much by what crime was committed but by his readiness to rejoin society. [Macdonald, 1958, p. 125]

In other words, what the state cannot do under civil commitment procedures it both can and should do under criminal procedures.[b] However, the psychiatrist, therapist and social worker have all been trained to draw exclusively on assumptions concerning problematic behavior totally independent of the socio-legal framework, thus necessarily obscuring the state's role in producing that behavior.

Since this responsibility of the state is several times removed from the actual conditions within which the inmate lives, the process whereby his problems are seen to be "within" his head is not too difficult to manage. One would think, however, that with regard to his *daily* conflicts with the custodians and managers of the prison, it would be difficult to convince him that indeed the environment is sterile, depriving, insecure, and generally neuroticizing because of something *he* does; far from this proving a real difficulty, however, it has provided material for his "cure."

It is worth noting at length the treatment of those inmates who "are not initially motivated to seek help because they do not see themselves as having real problems."

There are 7 stages in the treatment of those who refuse to psychologize their "problems." In the first stage, the inmate will try to manipulate the therapist:

> When the inmate fails to define the worker as a "dupe" or "sucker" he then tries to put him in the role of oppressor or "son of a bitch."

---

[b]The limits of due process protection from the courts should be apparent here.

Somewhere along here, the subject enters the second stage, in which he withdraws from therapy. . . . At this point, it is vital that the entire institution be able to thwart the prisoner in this kind of attempted adjustment, while at the same time allowing him sufficient freedom to try to establish an exploitive adjustment. *In other words, he must not be prevented from trying "to beat the system" but he must be made to fail at the attempt.* . . . After a time [which includes being placed in segregation when he inevitably becomes disruptive] the inmate would enter the fourth stage of despair . . . the stage of self-doubt emerges . . . the therapist would begin to help the offender. [Korn and McCorkle, 1959, pp. 540-552 as quoted by Gibbons (1965, p. 169; italics added]

So much for those who might think their problems are not in their heads. By the time the therapy is over, of course, it *is* in his head but at the hand of the therapist who is a paid employee of the state.

Obviously such programs must systematically ignore the meaning of the environment within which they operate. The usefulness of psychiatric tests must be as limited as the behaviorial possibilities available to the subjects on whom they are performed. The test used in our particular project[c] made much reference to fears of traveling, fears of feeling punished, sexual adjustments, and work adjustments. This is in an environment where travel consists of going from one's cell to the cafeteria and back to one's cell or work place across the yard; this is in an environment where one is constantly reminded that one is indeed being punished, where sexual adjustment means either masturbation, homosexuality, or a total reduction of sex drive, and where work assignments are almost totally a function of whether or not one is considered to be a security risk. We soon gave up the more blatantly ridiculous questions, but each and every question on our "objective" test smacked of a total callousness to the prisoner's actual situation. For example, we asked the following questions of inmates:

How are you getting along with people?
What kind of trouble do you have with people?
Who bothers or upsets you the most?
Whom do you feel you can trust the most?
Do you have much to do with (your neighbors, co-workers, students, the other people here)?
If no: why not?
Is there anybody that you visit with (here in the hospital)? [Cleverly we changed this last to "prison."]

---

[c]We purposefully do not reveal the name of the test used since we believe that this would be to single out for disparagement one effort that is no more responsible for the problems we met in its use than would have been true of any other such test.

If immediate family member: (anybody outside the family?)
How do you feel when you are with people?
How do people generally seem to feel about you?
How often do you and your friend(s) get together or keep in touch?

These questions come equipped with scoring guides. So we looked for the following, and if the inmate displayed these qualities we scored him as "true," which once fed into the computer objectively measured the extent of symptomology along this particular dimension.

Complains about the way peers of strangers treat him.
Complains unduly about the way people in positions of authority or
    power treat him (e.g., staff members, police, employer).
Indicates he cannot trust other people or that he is unduly suspicious
    of their intent.
Mentions he feels people take advantage of him or push him around.
Indicates that he often avoids or fears contact or involvements with
    (neighbors, co-workers, students, other people in the institution
    because of his psychopathology).
Indicates that he practically never visits anyone outside his immediate
    family.
Mentions he feels inhibited or uncomfortable with people.
Mentions he feels distant or isolated from people.
Mentions he stays by himself or likes to be alone.
Says he feels people avoid, reject, or dislike him.
Indicates he feels he has practically no friends.
Indicates he feels he has practically no friends or that he has little if
    any contact with his friends.

All of these symptoms add up to a picture of paranoia and suspicion. Consider, then, the character of the paranoic as depicted by responses to these questions. He complains about his treatment, feels that he cannot trust other people, has little or no contact with the external world of associates, and feels isolated from people. If he visits only with his family and has no friends, he registers on the computer as displaying some symptomology. Fewer than two good friends will also register as displaying some psychopathology.

It is not altogether surprising that a scale designed to measure a pattern of social relationships either forbidden or retarded by prison regulations will reveal that over 75 percent of those inmates tested will display some "pathology."

Szasz points out that to "see" a patient's statements about himself or his environment as a mental symptom involves rendering a judgement:

The judgment entails . . . a covert comparison or matching of the
patient's ideas, concepts, or beliefs with those of the observer

and the society in which they live. . . . Difficulties in human relations can be analyzed, interpreted, and given meaning only within
specific social and ethical contexts. [Szasz, 1963, pp. 13 and 15]

In the body of knowledge that makes up psychiatry and the other "helping" professions, this comparison is codified as a taken-for-granted world view.
Given the class that most of these professionals came from and the class of
patients for whom their training is leading them to treat, this "world view"
generally matches with the contexts of their patients' lives and within which
they express their problems. Unfortunately, it is also used in contexts that do
not meet these specifications—that is, the structures within which the prisoner
lives and experiences problems. (This, of course, is true for women and blacks
and has been noted as presenting a problem for psychiatry. Of course the problem is not that they live in peculiar environments but that the psychiatric knowledge is formed from the point of view of a very particular kind of environment
and then poses as being "value-free"—scientific.)

Immediately below these sets of questions is the section marked HUMOR
" How is your sense of humor?" "Says his sense of humor is poor OR that it is
not as good as usual." "If subject has not been observed to smile up to this
point, interviewer should smile and ask: Have you forgotten how to smile?"
"Does not smile either spontaneously or in response to suggestion." We have
no data on these items since we very quickly gave them up.

The very presence of those within the "helping" professions in the prison
either lent credence to the claim that the prison itself was merely an undiffer-
entiated background, without character or influence within which the inmate
acted out his problems; or it suggested that the prison was an environment that
was somehow affecting the inmate's existence but that the mandate of the
experts was directed at "curing" the inmate, which thus ratifies the belief that,
despite environmental pressures, the inmate still must be held fully accountable
for what he does or feels.

This last, of course, is precisely what is held by most "modern" prison
officials who, while blaming the environment from which he comes, "treat"
the offender in total disregard for that environment. We have suggested that
such a change in the ideological grounds of the prison serves to depoliticalize
the nature of crime while at the same time giving the state the authority necessary for controlling it.

If we are to take seriously the notion that crime is at root a political affair
and insofar as it (1) requires state control and legitimization and (2) therefore
rests on the political grounds that legitimize, state authority, then this increasing trend toward transforming politics into psychology must serve some purpose.
This social control exercized in the name of the "helping" professions, to
paraphrase Habermas [1970, p. 42] makes use of the spectacle of the under-
mined psyche of the inmate in order to make political processes unrecognizable

as such. The public realm of legitimate authority and responsibility of which crime is an inhering aspect becomes irrelevant and through psychologizing turns into privatism of the worst sort. The personalization of what is public is thus the cement in the cracks of a state whose claims for legitimacy no longer match social and economic conditions and which, therefore, forces political conflicts into areas of psychology.

8 Conclusion

The most common complaint heard about American prisons is that the constant flow of innovations intended to cure their many faults invariably become part of the original problem. We have argued that this failure of reform is traceable to the political genesis of crime and punishment.

This is not a statement about the influence of local, graft-seeking politicians or the parochial aims and interest of those in office. Rather, prisons are solely and totally a creation of the legal and political system. While public schools, hospitals, and orphanages are themselves creatures of state assemblies, private alternatives are found everywhere. No one, however, can imagine a "private" prison. In fact, what is done in prison is against the law if it is done anywhere else [Kennedy, 1970]. The sole difference between crime and punishment or criminal and custodian is a distinction provided by political arrangements. To the extent that these arrangements fail to conform to the justifications on which they are founded, the prison must mask that failure by creating ceremonies, methodologies, and ideologies to confirm the "fact" that the problem of the inmate is individual in origin and in need of public solution.

As the disjunction between inmate treatment and its corresponding social doctrine grows—as imprisonment looks increasingly inequitable—the state must convince its citizens of its social necessity despite its moral questionability. Various attempts at displaying the problem of "crime in the streets" (an attempt often made by gentlemen now under indictment) can be read as masking this inequity.

Other authors [Kadish, 1967, pp. 157-170] have commented on the problem of "overcriminalization" whereby the law is used to control the private lives of citizens. What we stress, however, is the "undercriminalization" of so many behaviors, which are often the source of the *greatest social danger* and which manage to receive the mildest penal sanction. When one recent effort [President's Commission II] was made to determine the extent of crime beyond what is reported to the police, "victimization" was defined solely in terms of one individual assaulting another individual. Totally ignored in this study was the extent (and even existence) of institutional assaults on whole social groups, the violence of racism, the violence of poverty and starvation, the violence of war, the violence of corporate or government pollution and so forth. This study is typical and its efforts are not simply incomplete. They are systematically misleading and in systematic ways. Of course there is general agreement that most crime does not land someone in jail. The effects of such studies, however, can be seen not as a simple affirmation of this perception, but as *guiding* the perception in selective ways—that is, they make us believe that the bulk of unimprisoned crime is traditional street crime—poor people's crime—the sort of crime for which most inmates are now behind bars. To the extent that this perception is packaged, sold, and consumed, we can be convinced that the inequity of differentially penalizing the mugger and the polluter is not the greatest source of judicial imbalance or even a serious one.

When we say that prisons are political institutions, we are saying that they directly reflect the overall power base of the society and, by implication, in order to change the former one must structurally transform the latter. And when we say that all inmates are political prisoners, we are not asserting that all criminal acts are deliberate, self-conscious acts of rebellion against an unjust authority. In fact, the overwhelming majority of inmates we saw are doing time for narrow, selfish acts such as stealing, breaking and entering, and fighting.

Nevertheless, their *incarceration* is political since it is the end-product of decisions to treat some social harms as deserving of penal sanction and others not—with little regard to the actual extent of social damage. It is foolish to assume that such politically induced decisions do not in the end favor one class at the expense of another. While the particular type of inmate may vary from state to state, the economic background remains constant; some prisons specialize in Mexican-Americans, some in native-Americans, most in Afro-Americans, and all in poor Americans.

We agree with the prison's "loyal opposition" that day-to-day prison conditions are horrid, squalid, and inhuman. Where we disagree is on the focus of and limits to reform. What reformers cannot take seriously is the *systematic* nature of these ills produced by the prison's intimate relation to the greater political and economic arrangements within which they function. Prison critics, then, have the obvious and inescapable mandate to attack the social parameters underlying incarceration. And there has been movement in this direction. But part of that movement has been deflected to experiments such as those associated with behavior modification programs, increased psychiatric care and special prisons for the special offender. The trait common to all such approaches is the obscuring of the prison's necessary relation to the state.

It is easy to see how the prison itself finds this deflection congenial and encourages it. For to understand the prison's structure, rituals, and daily treatment of inmates is to understand a political unit that must affirm a political doctrine that no longer reflects social or economic conditions. The support of an empty doctrine necessitates the convincing of prisoners that their selves are unworthy of full participation in a market society even though such a society is mythical. Inmates are expected to live up to social conditions that are absent from their personal experiences of the world.

In order to mask this fundamental divergence of theory and practice, the prison must insist that it is not the selective, discriminatory economic, and judicial environment that produces inmate "irrationality" but rather some disease of individual character. The prison, then, will model itself along treatment modalities and in the name of enlightened rehabilitative efforts will raise blind obedience to authority to the level of mental health and demote those incapable of such obedience to the level of the socially diseased. It will replace rationality with ritual, justice with "therapy," and its power will grow.

What is more distressing is the acceptance among those outside the prison of Patuxent-style experiments. How is it that the drive, so powerful in the last few decades, to identify environmental and economic factors as critical to the penal, vocational, and educational sectors, often ends up supporting a totally *individualized* method of social control? While the role of the theoretician should not be overestimated, the gentle critic has had some input.

If, as some of these critics maintain, *social* factors are so crucial and if the situation is so bleak, massive political changes are required. And aside from those in power who find this obviously unacceptable, many individuals for many reasons likewise back off at the crucial moment. Faced with an analysis whose bottom line could threaten the foundation of the work they have done in or around prisons, or which would threaten a political and social order they *do not fundamentally oppose*, the reformers substitute stereotypes of the individual for analysis of the general society.

Under the traditional punitive model, crime is an instance in which the society is right and has been wronged. The thrust of liberal reform is to see the offender as also being wronged, but at the same time *not himself right*. Victimized as he may be, he is still the offender, the defective. This perspective is summed up rather nicely in the apocryphal story about the white youngster who said, "We should not discriminate against Negroes and other inferior people." Despite decades of lip service, the predictable result of social and penal efforts remains at the individual level. And, of course, such efforts don't work. And, of course, similar though stronger measures are then justified. It is, in short, one more or less manageable step to rationalize and institutionalize experiments in enforced behavior modifications, aversion therapy and, in the most dire cases, psycho-surgery.

Such practices are relatively new and they have attracted much sharp criticism. But, if history is a guide, the bulk of that criticism will center on the excesses and specific cruelties of these procedures rather than on the substantive issue of the personalization of a social problem conjoined with the institutionalization of its solution.

The American prison system is a response to specific historical factors. Hence, isolated penal reform will always frustrate because it fails to deal with the social structure, which is the basic determining factor of that system. And to the extent that the prison is successful in incorporating ceremonies and ideologies that mask its political nature, the possibilities for raising consciousness and hence producing meaningful change are proportionately retarded.

This is not to suggest hopelessness, nor is it to counsel against specific political acts against various aspects of that system. In early 1974, for example, inmate and citizen resistance forced the government to close down its behavior modification program in Springfield, Missouri [*The New York Times*, Feb. 2, 1974]. While the government gave as its reasons "economic infeasibility" and said that it had not given up on the idea of behavior modification (the latter certainly being true), the fact remains that prisoner movements *can* be successful, if they are supported by "outsiders." Reform of this sort, where the inmates themselves rather than enlightened critics shape critical policy, is precisely the sort that has the potential for being part of the social transformation necessary to deal with the problems of the prison. The formation of prisoner unions and newsletters are among the most hopeful signs that such changes are in the wind. Such movements, in addition to all other social benefits they bring, transform the involved inmates into precisely the sort of individual the society claims it wants—autonomous, diligent, self-restrained, and responsible. And, of course, such movements are precisely those that receive the brunt of administrative and state disapproval. Such movements must be protected, strengthened, and allowed to flourish.

On the more general level, the fact that prisons are a creation of a particular political environment can be as much a cause for celebration as for despair. For a social institution profoundly rooted in a set of economic and political relations can be overcome by addressing those relations. And though the history of penal reformation is generally dismal, the one fact that stands out is the instability of any system based on falsified doctrine. Change is inevitable, but the decency of that change is very much a matter of political struggle. The outcome is as uncertain as the fact that the present social and penal systems cannot remain stationary is certain.

Uncomfortable as it may make us feel, there is nothing wrong with the forcible incarceration of serious wrongdoers. There is, however, everything in the world wrong with incarceration when it is based on class lines and interests and is unrelated to either social justice or social harm. A just prison in an unjust society is an illusion. Although prisons would be the exception rather than the rule, a just society would in all probability have them, but they would represent honest reactions to socially repugnant behavior. They would hide behind nothing. Prisons will only improve dramatically when a new political system in the process and eventual reality of becoming a just society with the strength of cast-off old doctrines, biases, and practices allows for that improvement. The prisoner movement in recent years is but one part of that new society. There are many others and their participants' interests and aims are converging.

But that is the beginning of a new story—the story of the gradual renewal of a man, the story of his gradual regeneration, of his passing from one world into another, of his initiation into a new unknown life. That might be the subject of a new story, but our present story is ended.

—Fyodor Dostoyevsky, *Crime and Punishment*

Bibliography

Bibliography

Agcock, William B., and Wurfel, W. *Law Under the Uniform Code of Military Justice.* Chapel Hill: University of North Carolina Press, 1955.

Appley, Mortimer H., and Trumbull, Fieford. *Psychological Stress.* New York: Appleton, Century and Crofts, 1967.

Armor, David, and Klerman, Gerald. "Psychiatric Treatment Orientations and Professional Ideology." *Journal of Health and Social Behavior,* Vol. 9, No. 3 (1968), pp. 243-255.

Attica: The Official Report of the New York State Special Commission on Attica. New York: Bantam Books, 1972.

Aubert, Vilholm. "Chance in Social Affairs." *Inquiry,* Vol. 2 (1959), pp. 1-24.

Bagdikian, Ben, and Dash, Leon. *The Shame of the Prisons.* New York: Pocket Books, 1972.

Banfield, Edward C. *The Unheavenly City.* Boston: Little, Brown and Co., 1968.

Baran, Paul, and Sweezy, Paul. *Monopoly Capital.* New York: Monthly Review Press, 1966.

Barnes, Harry E., and Teeters, Negley K. *New Horizons in Criminology.* 3rd ed. Englewood Cliffs, N.J.: Prentice-Hall, 1959.

Bayley, David, and Mendelsohn, Harold. *Minorities and the Police.* New York: Free Press, 1968.

Beaumont, G. de, and de Tocqueville, A. *On the Penitentiary System in the United States.* Philadelphia: Carney, Lea and Blanchard, 1883.

Beccaria, C.B. *An Essay on Crimes and Punishments.* London, 1762.

Becker, Howard S. *Outsiders: Studies in the Sociology of Deviance.* New York: The Free Press of Glencoe, 1963.

Berg, Ivan. *Education and Jobs: The Great Training Robbery.* New York: Praeger, 1970.

Bettleheim, Bruno. *The Informed Heart.* New York: The Free Press of Glencoe, 1960.

Blumberg, Abraham. *Criminal Justice.* Chicago: Quadrangle Books, 1967.

Bombard, Alain. *The Voyage of the Heretique.* New York: Simon and Schuster, 1954.

Bruner, J.S., and Goodman, C.D. "Value and Need as Organizing Factors in Perception." *Journal of Abnormal Social Psychology* 42 (1947): 33-44.

Bucher, Rue. "Vocabularies of Realism in Professional Socialization." Mimeographed.

Bureau of the Census. *Statistical Abstract of the United States.* 1972.

Burns, A.F. *The Frontiers of Economic Knowledge.* Princeton: Princeton University Press, 1954.

Carter, Robert; Glasser, Daniel; Wilkins, Leslie (eds.). *Correctional Institutions.* New York: J.B. Lippincott Co., 1972.

Chamber of Commerce. "Marshalling Citizen Power to Modernize Corrections." 1972.

Chambliss, William (ed.). *Sociological Readings in the Conflict Perspective.* Reading, Mass.: Addison-Wesley Publishing Co., 1973.

Chambliss, William J. "Elites and the Creation of Criminal Law." *Sociological Readings in the Conflict Perspective.* Reading, Mass.: Addison-Wesley Publishing Co., 1973.

Cloward, Richard. "Social Control in the Prisons." An unpublished paper read at the meeting of the Social Science Research Conference on Research in Correctional Organizations. February 1956.

Cohen, Albert K. *Delinquent Boys.* New York: The Free Press, 1955.

Cohen, Arthur R. *Attitude Change and Social Influence.* New York: Basic Books, Inc., 1964.

Cohen, Stanley, and Taylor, Laurie. *Psychological Survival; The Experience of Long Term Imprisonment.* Harmondsworth, Middlesex, England: Penguin Books, Ltd., 1972.

Connolly, William. "Comment on Bay's 'The Liberal Make-Believe.' " *Inquiry,* Vol. 14 (1971), p. 246.

Creesy, Donald R. "Archievement of an Unstated Organizational Goal." *Complex Organizations.* Edited by Amitai Etzioni. New York: Holt, Rinehart and Winston, 1961.

Creesy, Donald. *Delinquency, Crime and Differential Association.* The Hague: Martinus Nijhoff, 1964.

Curran, Dr. William J. *A Feasibility Study for the Development of New England Programs for the Management and Treatment of Dangerous Social Offenders.* Boston, Mass.: Socio-Technical Systems, November 26, 1973.

Dahl, Robert, and Lindblom, Charles. *Politics, Economies and Welfare.* New York: Harper and Row, 1953.

de Jouvenel, Bertrand. *On Power.* New York: Viking Press, 1949.

de Tocqueville, Alexis. "Of Individualism in Democratic Countries." *Democracy in America.* London: Saunders and Otley, 1840.

de Tracy, Antoine Louis. *A Commentary and Review of Montesquieu's Spirit of Laws.* Philadelphia, 1811.

Edwards, Newton. *The Courts and the Public Schools: The Legal Basis of School Organization and Administration.* 3rd. ed. Chicago: University of Chicago Press, 1971.

Elliott, Phillip. *The Sociology of the Professions.* New York: Herder and Herder, 1972.

Emerging Rights of the Confined, The. Columbia, S.C.: South Carolina Department of Corrections, 1972.

Erikson, Erik. "The Problem of Ego Identity." *Journal of American Psychoanalytic Association,* IV, No. 1 (1956), pp. 58-121.

Etzioni, Amitai. *Modern Organizations.* Englewood Cliffs, N.J.: Prentice-Hall, 1964.

Fanon, Franz. *The Wretched of the Earth.* New York: Grove Press, 1963.

Faulkner, William. *Light in August.* New York: Harrison, Smith and Robert Haas, 1932.

Federal Bureau of Prisons. *National Prisoner Statistics,* 1970.

Fischer, Bernice M. "Claims and Credibility: A Discussion of Occupational Identity and the Agent Client Relationship." *Social Problems,* Vol. 16, No. 4 (Spring 1969), pp. 423-433.

Fisher, J. *The Art of Detection.* Sterling Paperbacks, 1961.

Fletcher, F.T.H. *Montesquieu and English Politics.* London: Edward Arnold and Co., 1939.

Freidson, Elliot. *The Social Organization of Medicine.* New York: Dodd, Mead, 1970.

Friedman, Bruce Jay. *The Dick.* New York: Alfred Knopf, 1971.

Fromm, Eric. *The Sane Society.* New York: Reinhart, 1955.

Gagnon, John, and Simon, William. "The Social Meaning of Prison Homosexuality." In Carter, Robert; Glaser, Daniel; and Wilkins, Leslie. *Correctional Institutions.* New York: J.B. Lippincott, 1972, pp. 221-231.

Gibbons, Don C. Changing the Lawbreaker, The Treatment of *Delinquents and Criminals.* Englewood Cliffs, N.J.: Prentice-Hall, 1965.

Glaser, Daniel. "Disciplinary Action and Counseling." In Carter, Robert; Glaser, Daniel; and Wilkins, Leslie. *Correctional Institutions.* New York: J.B. Lippincott Co., 1972, pp. 329-339.

Goebel, Julius, and Naughton, T. Raymond. *Law Enforcement in Colonial New York.* New York: The Commonwealth Fund, 1944.

Goffman, Erving. *Behavior in Public Places.* New York: The Free Press, 1963.

―――. "Alienation from Interaction." *Human Relations,* Vol. 10 (1957), pp. 47-60.

―――. *Asylums.* Garden City, N.Y.: Doubleday, 1961.

―――. *Strategic Interaction.* Pennsylvania: University of Pennsylvania Press, 1969.

Gouldner, Alvin. 'Metaphysical Pathos and Bureaucracy." *American Political Science Review,* Vol. 59 (1955), pp. 496-507.

Greer, Edward. "The Public Interest University." *Economics: Mainstream Readings and Radical Critiques.* Edited by David Mermelstein. New York: Random House, 1970.

Grinker, Roy R., and Spiegel, John P. *Men Under Stress.* Philadelphia: Blakiston, 1945.

Gusfield, Joseph. *Symbolic Crusade: Status Politics and the American Temperance Movement.* Urbana, Ill.: University of Illinois Press, 1963.

Habermas, Jurgin. *Toward a Rational Society.* Boston: Beacon Press, 1970.

Halleck, Seymour. *Psychiatry and the Dilemmas of Crime.* New York: Harper and Row, 1967.

Halmos, Paul. *Solitude and Privacy.* New York: Greenwood Press, 1953.

Haney, Bill, Martin, Gold. "The Juvenile Deliquent Nobody Knows." *Psychology Today,* September 1973.

Hart, H.L.A. *Punishment and Responsibility.* New York: Oxford University Press, 1968.

Heilbroner, Robert. *The Making of Economic Society*. Englewood Cliffs:
    Prentice-Hall, 1962.
H.E.W. *Task Force on Work in America*. Washington, D.C.: U.S. Government
    Printing Office, 1973.
Hickey, William L. *Civil Commitment of Special Category of Offenders*.
    Rockville, Maryland: National Institute of Mental Health, Center for
    Studies of Crime and Delinquency, n.d.
Hobbes, Thomas. *Leviathen*. Reprinted from the edition of 1651. Oxford
    1909.
Hughes, Everett C. "Good People and Dirty Work." *Social Problems*, Vol. 10
    (1962-63), pp. 3-11.
Indeterminate Sentence, The. New York: United Nations Department of
    Social Affairs, 1954.
Ives, George. *A History of Penal Methods*. New York: Fredrich Stokes
    Company, 1915.
Jackson, George. *Soledad Brother*. New York: Coward-McCann, Inc., 1970.
Kadish, Sanford, H. "The Crisis of Overcriminalization." *Annals*, 374
    (November 1967).
Kaufman, Arnold S. "Wants, Needs and Liberalism." *Inquiry*, Vol. 14 (1971),
    pp. 191-206.
Kennedy, Mark C. "Beyond Incrimination." *Catalyst* (Summer, 1970),
    pp. 1-37.
Kolko, Gabriel. *The Triumph of Conservatism*. Chicago: Quadrangle Books,
    1963.
Korn, Richard, F., and McCorkle, Lloyd W. *Criminology and Penology*. New
    York: Holt, Rinehart & Winston, Inc., 1959.
Kuhn, Thomas S. *The Structure of Scientific Revolutions*. 2nd ed. Chicago:
    University of Chicago Press, 1970.
Laing, R.D. *The Divided Self*. Baltimore: Penguin Books, 1965.
Lemert, E. *Social Pathology: A Systemic Approach to the Theory of Socio-
    pathic Behavior*. New York: McGraw-Hill, 1951.
Lenski, Gerhard. *Power and Privilege*. New York: McGraw-Hill, 1966.
Light, Donald W. "Psychiatry and Suicide: The Management of a Mistake."
    American Journal of Sociology, 77 (March 1972).
Lindner, Robert. "Sexual Behavior in Penal Institutions." *Sex Habits of
    American Men*. Edited by Albert Deutsch. New York: Prentice-Hall,
    1948.
Lofland, John. *Deviance and Identity*. Englewood Cliffs, N.J.: Prentice-Hall,
    Inc., 1969.
Luparar. Vermont State Prisoner's Newsletter. 1972.
MacDonald, John M. *Psychiatry and the Criminal*. Springfield, Ill.: Charles C.
    Thomas, 1958.
MacPherson, C.B. *The Political Theory of Possessive Individualism*. Oxford:
    Clarendon Press, 1962.
Manual for Courts Martial. U.S., 1951.
Manual of Correctional Standards. Washington, D.C.: American Correctional
    Association, 1966.

Mattick, Hans. "The Prosaic Sources of Prison Violence." *Occasional Papers from the Law School*. Chicago: The University of Chicago Press, March 1972.

Matza, David. *Delinquency and Drift*. New York: John Wiley and Sons, Inc., 1964.

Metcalf, Lee and Reinemer, Vic. *Overcharge*. New York: David McKay Company, 1967.

Mitford, Jessica. *Kind and Unusual Punishment*. New York: Alfred Knopf, 1973.

Mulbar, H. *Interrogation*. Springfield: Charles Thomas, 1951.

Murphy, Jeffrie G. "Marxism and Retribution." *Philosophy and Public Affairs*. 1973.

Nettler, Gwynn. *Explaining Crime*. New York: McGraw-Hill, 1974.

New England Prisoner Association News. November 1973.

New University Conference. "Classes and Schools: A Radical Definition for Teachers." 1971. Mimeographed.

O'Neill, John. *Sociology as a Skin Trade*. New York: Harper, 1972.

Oswald, Russell. *Attica, My Story*. New York: Doubleday and Co., 1972.

Pitts, J.R. "Introduction." *Theories of Society*. Vol. II. Edited by Talcott Parsons, Edward Shils, K.D. Naegele, and J.R. Pitts. New York: The Free Press of Glencoe, 1961.

President's Commission on Law Enforcement and Administration of Justice, The. *Task Force Report: Corrections*. Washington, D.C.: U.S. Government Printing Office, 1967.

President's Commission II on Law Enforcement and Administration of Justice. *Task Force Report: Crime and Its Impact—An Assessment*. Washington, D.C.: U.S. Government Printing Office, 1967.

Radzinowicz, Leon. *Crime and Ideology*. New York: Columbia University Press, 1966.

Report of the Penitentiaries of the United States. London, 1935.

Roth, Julius. *Time Tables*. New York: Bobbs-Merrill, 1968.

Rothman, David. *The Discovery of the Asylum*. Boston: Little, Brown and Co., 1971.

Rothstein, Richard. "Down the Up Staircase: Tracking in Schools." A New University Conference Publication, 1971. Mimeographed.

Rubinstein, Jonathan. *City Police*. New York: Farrar, Straus, and Giroux, 1973.

Rusche, Georg, and Kirchheimer, Otto. *Punishment and Social Structure*. New York: Columbia University Press, 1939.

Ryan, William. *Blaming the Victim*. New York: Pantheon Books, 1971.

Schein, Edgar. "Interpersonal Communication, Group Solidarity and Social Influence." *Sociometry*, 23 (1960-61): 148-161.

Schwitzgebel, Ralph K. *Development and Legal Regulation of Coercive Behavior Modification Techniques with Offenders*. Chevy Chase, Md.: National Institutes of Mental Health Center for Studies of Crime and Delinquency, 1971.

Select Committee on the Administration of Justice. "Order Out of Chaos." Washington, D.C., 1970.

Sellin, Thorstein. "Filippo-Franci—A Precursor of Modern Penology." *Journal of Criminal Law and Criminology*, XVII (1926), pp. 104-112.

Seymour, Whitney North. *Why Justice Fails*. New York: William Morrow & Co., 1973.

Shaw, A.G.L. *Convicts and Colonies*. London: Faber & Faber, 1966.

Sheatsley, Paul B., and Feldman, Jacob J. "The Assassination of President Kennedy: A Preliminary Report on Public Reactions and Behavior." *Public Opinion Quarterly*, Vol. 28, No. 2 (1964), pp. 189-215.

Simmel, George. *Edited Works*. Kurt Wolfe (ed.). Glencoe, Ill.: The Free Press, 1950.

Sommer, Robert. *Expertland*. New York: Doubleday & Co., Inc., 1963.

Special Committee to Study Commitment Procedures. *Mental Illness and Due Process: Report and Recommendations on Admission to Mental Hospitals Under New York Law*. Ithaca, N.Y.: Cornell University Press, 1962.

Spenser, P.S. *Theologische Bedenken*. 3d ed., 1712.

State of Vermont, Department of Corrections Biennial Report, for the Two Years Ending June 30, 1970.

Street, David; Vinter, R.D.; and Perrow, Charles. *Organization for Treatment*. Glencoe, Ill.: The Free Press, 1966.

Sudnow, David. "Normal Crimes: Sociological Features of the Penal Code in a Public Defender's Office." *Social Problems*, 12 (1964, 65), pp. 255-276.

Sullivan, Henry Stack. "A Note on the Implications of Psychiatry in the Study of Interpersonal Relations for Investigations in the Social Sciences." *American Journal of Sociology* Vol. XLII, No. 6 (1936-37), pp. 848-861.

Sykes, Greshan. "The Corruption of Authority and Rehabilitation." *Social Forces*, Vol. 34, No. 3 (March 1956), pp. 257-262.

Sykes, Greshan. *The Society of Captives: A Study of a Maximum Security Prison*. Princeton, N.J.: Princeton University Press, 1958.

Szasz, Thomas S. *Law, Liberty and Psychiatry*. New York: The Macmillan Co., 1963.

Tawney, R.H. *Religion and the Rise of Capitalism*. New York: New American Library, 1954.

Tobias, J.J. *Crime and Industrial Society in the 19th Century*. New York: Schocken Books, 1967.

U.S. Bureau of Prisons. *Characteristics of State Prisoners*. 1965.

Utpon, Lettia, and Lyons, Nancy. "Basic Facts on Distribution of Income and Personal Wealth." Cambridge, Mass.: The Cambridge Institute, 1970.

von Hentig, Hans. *Punishment: Its Origins, Purpose and Psychology*. London: William Hodge & Co., 1937.

Weber, Max. *General Economic History*. New York: Greenberg, 1927.

_____. *On Law in Economy and Society*. New York: Simon and Schuster, 1967.

Weinstein, James. *The Corporate Ideal in the Liberal State 1900-1918*. Boston: Beacon Press, 1969.

Wittfogel, Karl. *Oriental Despotism: A Comparative Study of Total Power* New Haven: Yale University Press, 1957.

Wooten, Barbara. *Social Science and Social Pathology.* London: Allen and Unwin, 1959.

Zola, Irving. "Medicine As An Institution of Social Control." *Sociological Review,* Vol. 20, No. 4 (New Series; November 1972).

Index

Index

About the Authors

Joan Smith is Assistant Professor of Sociology at Dartmouth College. She received the B.A. from Roosevelt University, the M.S. from Illinois Institute of Technology, and the Ph.D. from New York University. She is working on a book concerning the political implications of the work of B.F. Skinner and Noam Chomsky.

William Fried is Visiting Lecturer in Philosophy at Dartmouth College. He received the B.A. from the University of Pittsburgh and the M.A. from Brown University. He is working on a book on the political economy of ecology.

DATE DUE

NOV 1 4 1980			
JUL 15			
JUN 1 0 1988			
MAR. 2 7 1985			
GAYLORD			PRINTED IN U.S.A.